Pocket
ROME

TOP SIGHTS • LOCAL LIFE • MADE EASY

Duncan Garwood

In This Book

QuickStart Guide

Your keys to understanding the city – we help you decide what to do and how to do it

Need to Know
Tips for a smooth trip

Neighbourhoods
What's where

Explore Rome

The best things to see and do, neighbourhood by neighbourhood

Top Sights
Make the most of your visit

Local Life
The insider's city

The Best of Rome

The city's highlights in handy lists to help you plan

Best Walks
See the city on foot

Rome's Best...
The best experiences

Survival Guide

Tips and tricks for a seamless, hassle-free Rome experience

Getting Around
Travel like a local

Essential Information
Including where to stay

Our selection of the city's best places to eat, drink and experience:

◉ **Sights**

✖ **Eating**

◎ **Drinking**

★ **Entertainment**

🔒 **Shopping**

These symbols give you the vital information for each listing:

☏ Telephone Numbers	☗ Family-Friendly
⊙ Opening Hours	☗ Pet-Friendly
P Parking	☗ Bus
⊘ Nonsmoking	⊼ Ferry
@ Internet Access	M Metro
⊛ Wi-Fi Access	S Subway
☑ Vegetarian Selection	☗ Tram
◧ English-Language Menu	☗ Train

Find each listing quickly on maps for each neighbourhood:

Bar Hemingway

16 ◎ Map p233, B2

Legend has it that Hemi
self, wielding a machine
-rate this timber-pan
-ered bar during
showpiece is a
-n by Papa ar
town. Dress
s.com; Hôtel Rit
⊙6.30pm-2a

Lonely Planet's Rome

Lonely Planet Pocket Guides are designed to get you straight to the heart of the city.

Inside you'll find all the must-see sights, plus tips to make your visit to each one really memorable. We've split the city into easy-to-navigate neighbourhoods and provided clear maps so you'll find your way around with ease. Our expert authors have searched out the best of the city: walks, food, nightlife and shopping, to name a few. Because you want to explore, our 'Local Life' pages will take you to some of the most exciting areas to experience the real Rome.

And of course you'll find all the practical tips you need for a smooth trip: itineraries for short visits, how to get around, and how much to tip the guy who serves you a drink at the end of a long day's exploration.

It's your guarantee of a really great experience.

Our Promise

You can trust our travel infor-mation because Lonely Planet authors visit the places we write about, each and every edition. We never accept freebies for positive coverage, so you can rely on us to tell it like it is.

QuickStart Guide 7

Rome Top Sights............**8**
Rome Local Life............**12**
Rome Day Planner............**14**
Need to Know............**16**
Rome Neighbourhoods....**18**

Explore Rome 21

22	Ancient Rome
36	Centro Storico
54	Tridente
66	Trevi & the Quirinale
80	Monti & Esquilino
96	San Giovanni & Celio
108	Aventino & Testaccio
116	Trastevere & Gianicolo
130	Vatican City & Prati

Worth a Trip:

San Lorenzo & Pigneto............**78**
Appian Way............**92**
Ostiense & San Paolo............**106**
Villa Borghese............**146**

The Best of Rome 151

Rome's Best Walks

Emperors' Footsteps **152**

Piazzas of Rome **154**

Rome's Best...

History **156**

Food **158**

For Free **160**

Bars & Nightlife **161**

Architecture **162**

Art & Museums **164**

Shopping **166**

Culture **168**

For Kids **170**

Tours **171**

Gay & Lesbian **172**

Survival Guide 173

Before You Go **174**

Arriving in Rome **176**

Getting Around **177**

Essential Information **179**

Language **184**

Quickstart Guide

Rome Top Sights 8

Rome Local Life..................................... 12

Rome Day Planner................................. 14

Need to Know 16

Rome Neighbourhoods 18

Welcome to Rome

An epic, monumental city, Italy's hot-blooded capital gets under your skin fast. Even on a short break, you'll be bowled over by its awe-inspiring art and iconic ruins, baroque piazzas and vibrant street life. Cafes and neighbourhood trattorias hum with activity, while chic boutiques showcase the latest fashions and bars buzz into the small hours. Visit once and you'll be hooked for life.

Outdoor dining in Trastevere (p116)
BORIS-B/GETTY IMAGES ©

Rome
Top Sights

Colosseum (p24)

Rome's most iconic monument, the Colosseum is an electrifying sight. An architectural tour de force, it has been drawing the crowds since it first staged gladiatorial combat in the 1st century AD.

PAOLO CIPRIANI/GETTY IMAGES ©

Vatican Museums (p132)

This colossal museum complex boasts some of the world's most celebrated works of art, including Raphael's *La scuola di Atene* (The School of Athens) and Michelangelo's Sistine Chapel frescoes.

Pantheon (p38)

Rome's best-preserved ancient monument, this revolutionary building is one of the great masterpieces of Western architecture. Its design and record-breaking dome have been inspiring visitors for centuries, and it remains a thrilling sight.

St Peter's Basilica (p136)

The most important church in the Catholic world, St Peter's is Rome's largest and most spectacular basilica. Behind the grandiose facade, priceless artworks litter its lavish marble-clad interior.

Villa Borghese (p146)

Rome's central park harbours a host of attractions, including the superb Museo e Galleria Borghese, whose priceless collection contains works by Bernini, Caravaggio, Canova, Raphael and Titian.

Museo Nazionale Romano: Palazzo Massimo alle Terme (p82)

This is one of Rome's less-heralded highlights, full of heavyweight classical sculpture and some impressive ancient mosaics.

Appian Way (p92)

Flanked by green fields and umbrella pine trees, Via Appia Antica, the queen of ancient roads, has a morbid history – Spartacus was crucified here, and the early Christians buried their dead in the catacombs.

Roman Forum (p26)

Walk in the footsteps of Augustus, Julius Caesar, and other legends of Roman history as you explore the tumbledown ruins of the Roman Forum, once the glittering heart of the Roman Empire.

Spanish Steps & Piazza di Spagna (p56)

The Spanish Steps have provided a perch for tourists and poseurs since the 18th century. There are memorable rooftop views from the top and a carnival atmosphere on the piazza below.

Basilica di San Giovanni in Laterano (p98)

Officially Rome's main cathedral, this echoing, landmark basilica is the city's oldest, dating to the dog days of the Roman Empire. Inside and out, it's a memorable sight.

Basilica di Santa Maria in Trastevere (p118)

Discreetly tucked away on a charming piazza, this low-key looker was built on the site where an ancient miracle took place, and features some extraordinary 12th-century mosaics.

Trevi Fountain (p68)

A favourite film backdrop, Rome's best-known fountain is a gloriously over-the-top affair. Visitors flock here to toss a coin into the water and ensure they'll return to Rome.

Rome Local Life

Insider tips to help you find the real city

It's easy to be blinded by Rome's beauty, but scratch beneath the surface and you'll discover another side to the city. Here we explore the city's alternative hang-outs and boho bar haunts, its hot clubs and off-the-radar neighbourhoods.

A Day Out in the Centro Storico (p40)

▶ Beautiful backdrops
▶ Shopping and pizza

Once you've covered the centre's headline sights, it's time to slow down and enjoy the area like the locals do – catch an exhibition, shop for jeans, dine on pizza and beer.

San Lorenzo & Pigneto (p78)

▶ Bohemian bars
▶ Alternative art

Head to graffiti-clad San Lorenzo and boho Pigneto to admire one of

Rome's major basilicas, catch some contemporary art, and revel in laid-back nightlife. Join fashion-conscious diners at smart restaurants and drink cocktails at cool bars.

Ostiense & San Paolo (p106)

▶ Cool clubs
▶ Hidden culture

With its disused factories, street art, and university campus, Ostiense is home to Rome's hottest clubs and hippest bars. But before the nightlife revs up, you can explore several

fascinating cultural gems and the characterful Garbatella neighbourhood.

A Night Out in Trastevere & Gianicolo (p120)

▶ Views and heaving bars
▶ Basement blues

A picturesque district full of bars, cafes and trattorias, Trastevere has long been a foreigner favourite. But Romans love it, too, and amid the tourist bustle you'll find some characteristic city haunts.

Trastevere (p120)

Restaurant blackboard

PIZZA

- Farine macinate a Pietra 100% Bio!
- Ingredienti di Stagione di origine Laziale
- Lunga maturazione

• Pizza Gourmet

◦ Vegana
◦ Cacio e pepe · Sriracha
◦ crema di fave, pecorino e guanciale
◦ Parmigiana di spinaci
◦ Estrema di carciofi

Other great places to experience the city like a local:

Jewish Ghetto (p46)

Via Margutta (p59)

Piazza del Quirinale (p71)

Via del Boschetto (p90)

Pasticceria Regoli (p88)

Trastevere, Festa de' Noantri (p124)

Pastificio (p64)

Monte Testaccio (p112)

Rome
Day Planner

Day One

With only one day, start by getting to grips with the city's ancient wonders. Kick off at the **Colosseum** (p24) – get there early to avoid the worst queues – then head on to the **Palatino** (p31) to poke around crumbling ruins and admire sweeping views. From the Palatino follow the path down into the **Roman Forum** (p26), an evocative area of tumble-down temples and sprouting columns.

After an early lunch at **Terre e Domus** (p33), climb up to **Piazza del Campidoglio** (p31) and the **Capitoline Museums** (p31) where you'll find some stunning ancient sculpture. Done there, push onto the *centro storico* (historic centre) to explore its labyrinthine medieval streets and headline sights such as the **Pantheon** (p38) and **Piazza Navona** (p44).

Enjoy a romantic dinner at **Casa Coppelle** (p47) before getting a taste of *dolce vita* bar life. Depending on what you're after you could hang out with the beautiful people at **Etablì** (p50), chat over coffee at **Caffè Sant'Eustachio** (p50), or sup beer at **No.Au** (p51).

Day Two

On day two, hit the Vatican. First stop is the colossal **Vatican Museums** (p132). Once you've blown your mind on the Sistine Chapel and the many other highlights, complete your tour at **St Peter's Basilica** (p136). If you have the energy, climb its Michelangelo-designed **dome** (p138) for fantastic views over **St Peter's Square** (p142). Afterwards, grab a slice of gourmet pizza at **Pizzarium** (p142) or a slap-up trattoria meal at **Velavevo-detto Ai Quiriti** (p143).

Recharged, jump on the metro and head back over the river to check out **Piazza di Spagna** (p56). Plan your moves while sitting on the **Spanish Steps** and then push on to the **Trevi Fountain** (p68) where tradition dictates you throw a coin into the water to ensure your return to Rome. Next, head up the hill to catch the sunset on **Piazza del Quirinale** (p71) in front of the presidential palace, **Palazzo del Quirinale** (p72).

Spend the evening in the buzzing area around **Campo de' Fiori** (p46). Dine at **Ditirambo** (p49), a popular modern trattoria, then join the cool crowd at **Barnum Cafe** (p50) for cocktails and laid-back tunes.

Short on time?
We've arranged Rome's must-sees into these day-by-day itineraries to make sure you see the very best of the city in the time you have available.

Day Three

☀ Day three starts with a trip to the **Museo e Galleria Borghese** (p147) – don't forget to book – to marvel at amazing baroque sculpture. Afterwards, stroll through **Villa Borghese** (p146) down to the **Galleria Nazionale d'Arte Moderna e Contemporanea** (p148) for an injection of modern art. Lunch at the gallery's elegant cafe, the **Caffè delle Arti** (p147).

☀ In the afternoon, check what's going on at Rome's buzzing cultural centre, the **Auditorium Parco della Musica** (p148), before heading back to **Piazza del Popolo** (p59). Just off the piazza, the **Chiesa di Santa Maria del Popolo** (p59) is a magnificent repository of art. Next, dedicate some time to browsing the flagship stores and designer boutiques in the upscale streets off **Via del Corso** (p77).

☾ Over the river, the picture-perfect Trastevere neighbourhood bursts with life in the evening as locals and tourists flock to its many eateries and bars. Get into the mood with an *aperitivo* (bar buffet) at **Freni e Frizioni** (p121) before dining on Roman soul food at **Da Olindo** (p121) or something more refined at **Glass Hostaria** (p125).

Day Four

☀ On day four it's time to venture out to the **Appian Way** (p92) and the wonderfully creepy catacombs such as the **Catacombe di San Sebastiano** (p93). Above ground, you'll find the remains of an ancient racetrack in the grounds of **Villa di Massenzio** (p93). For lunch, stop off at the rustic **Qui Non se More Mai** (p93).

☀ Once you've eaten, head back to Stazione Termini and the nearby **Museo Nazionale Romano: Palazzo Massimo alle Terme** (p82), a superb museum full of classical sculpture and stunning mosaics. Then, drop by the monumental **Basilica di Santa Maria Maggiore** (p85), famous for its mosaics, and the **Basilica di San Pietro in Vincoli** (p85), home to Michelangelo's muscular *Moses* sculpture. Continue on down to the charming Monti district for some fashionable **shopping** (p90).

☾ Stay put in Monti, where there's plenty of late-night action. Dine on meaty Umbrian fare at the excellent **L'Asino d'Oro** (p87) and then take your pick of wine bar or cafe to see out the day; **Ai Tre Scalini** (p89) is a popular local choice.

Need to Know

For more information, see Survival Guide (p173)

Currency
Euro (€)

Language
Italian

Visas
Not required by EU citizens. Not required by nationals of Australia, Canada, New Zealand and the USA for stays of up to 90 days.

Money
ATMs are widespread. Major credit cards are widely accepted but some smaller shops and trattorias may not take them. Keep cash for immediate expenses.

Mobile Phones
Local SIM cards can be used in European, Australian and unlocked US phones. Other phones must be set to roaming.

Time
Western European Time (GMT/UTC plus one hour)

Plugs & Adaptors
Plugs have two or three round pins; electricity is 220V to 230V; North American travellers will require an adaptor and transformer.

Tipping
Not obligatory, but round up the bill in pizzerias or leave a euro or two; 10% is normal in upmarket restaurants.

① Before You Go

Your Daily Budget

Budget less than €100
► Dorm bed €15 to €35
► Pizza plus beer €15
► Drink coffee standing at the bar

Midrange €100 to €250
► Double room €110 to €200
► Three-course restaurant meal €25 to €50
► Roma Pass, a three-day card covering museum entry and public transport €36

Top End over €250
► Double room €200 plus
► Top restaurant dinner €50 to €150
► City taxi ride €10 to €15
► Auditorium concert tickets €25 to €90

Useful Websites

► **Lonely Planet** (www.lonelyplanet.com/rome) Planning info, hotels and traveller forum.

► **060608** (www.060608.it) Information on sights, accommodation, shows, transport etc.

► **Coop Culture** (www.coopculture.it) Information and ticketing for Rome's monuments, museums and galleries.

► **Vatican** (www.vatican.va) Book tickets for the Vatican Museums.

Advance Planning

► **Two months before** Book high-season rooms.

► **One to two weeks before** Reserve tables at A-list restaurants. Sort out tickets to the pope's weekly audience at the Vatican.

► **A few days before** Phone for tickets for the Museo e Galleria Borghese and book for the Vatican Museums.

② Arriving in Rome

Most visitors arrive at one of Rome's two airports: Leonardo da Vinci, also known as Fiumicino; or Ciampino, the hub for European low-cost carrier Ryanair – see www.adr.it. International trains serve Stazione Termini in the city centre.

✈ From Leonardo da Vinci (Fiumicino) Airport

Destination	Best Transport
Monti & Esquilino	Leonardo Express train, then metro line A or B
Centro Storico	Leonardo Express train, then bus 40 or 64
Trastevere	FL1 train, then tram 8
Vatican	Leonardo Express train, then metro line A; SIT bus
Tridente	Leonardo Express train, then metro line A

✈ From Ciampino Airport

Destination	Best Transport
Monti & Esquilino	Terravision/SIT bus, then metro line A or B
Centro Storico	Terravision/SIT bus, then bus 40 or 64
Trastevere	Terravision/SIT bus, then bus H
Vatican	Terravision/SIT bus, then metro line A
Tridente	Terravision/SIT bus, then metro line A

🚌 From Stazione Termini

Airport buses and trains, and international trains, arrive at Stazione Termini. From here you can take metro line A or B or hop on a bus to all main neighbourhoods. Taxis are available outside the main entrance.

③ Getting Around

Public transport is cheap and reasonably efficient, although occasional strikes can cause chaos. Buy a 24-/48-/72-hour pass to save time and money. For information and a route planner, see www.atac.roma.it.

Ⓜ Metro

The metro is the quickest way of getting around central Rome, although it's of limited use for the *centro storico* (historic centre). Lines A (orange) and B (blue) traverse the city in an X-shape, crossing at Stazione Termini. Services run from 5.30am to 11.30pm (to 1.30am on Fridays and Saturdays).

🚌 Bus

Chaotic traffic can slow buses, but they are still the best bet for the *centro storico*. The main bus station is in front of Stazione Termini on Piazza dei Cinquecento. Buses run from 5.30am until midnight, with limited services throughout the night. Remember to validate tickets in the yellow machines on board.

🚋 Tram

Tram 8 is the most useful, connecting the centre with Trastevere over the river. Trams are also useful for San Lorenzo and Pigneto.

🚕 Taxi

Taxis are useful late at night when bus services are slow and the metro has closed. Pick one up at a rank or call a taxi company direct. Surcharges apply after 10pm and for carrying luggage.

Rome
Neighbourhoods

Tridente (p54)
Designer stores and swanky bars set the tone for this stylish, upmarket district centred on two striking piazzas.

👁 **Top Sights**

Spanish Steps & Piazza di Spagna

Vatican City & Prati (p130)
Feast on extravagant art in the monumental Vatican and excellent food in neighbouring Prati.

👁 **Top Sights**

St Peter's Basilica

Vatican Museums

Centro Storico (p36)
Rome's historic centre is the capital's thumping heart – a heady warren of famous squares and tangled lanes, galleries, restaurants and bars.

👁 **Top Sights**

Pantheon

Trastevere & Gianicolo (p116)
Trastevere's medieval streets heave with kicking bars and eateries. The Gianicolo offers to-die-for panoramas.

👁 **Top Sights**

Basilica di Santa Maria in Trastevere

Ancient Rome (p22)
Rome's ancient core is a beautiful area of evocative ruins, improbable legends, soaring pine trees and panoramic views.

👁 **Top Sights**

Colosseum

Roman Forum

Villa Borghese

Vatican Museums

Spanish Steps & Piazza di Spagna

St Peter's Basilica

Trevi Fountain

Pantheon

Basilica di Santa Maria in Trastevere

Roman Forum

Trevi & the Quirinale (p66)

A busy, hilly district, home to Rome's most famous fountain, Italy's presidential palace and several stellar art galleries.

⊙ Top Sights

Trevi Fountain

Monti & Esquilino (p80)

Boutiques and wine bars abound in Monti, while Esquilino offers multiculturalism and several must-see museums and churches.

⊙ Top Sights

Museo Nazionale Romano: Palazzo Massimo alle Terme

⊙ Museo Nazionale Romano: Palazzo Massimo alle Terme

⊙ Colosseum

⊙ Basilica di San Giovanni in Laterano

Aventino & Testaccio (p108)

Ideal for a romantic getaway, hilltop Aventino rises above Testaccio, famous for its nose-to-tail cooking and thumping nightlife.

San Giovanni & Celio (p96)

Explore medieval churches and escape the tourist crowds in residential San Giovanni and on the leafy Celio hill.

⊙ Top Sights

Basilica di San Giovanni in Laterano

⊙ Appian Way

Worth a Trip

⊙ Top Sights

Appian Way

Villa Borghese

IV
V
VI
VII

VIII
IX
X

EXCELSA FILIA
SION

Explore
Rome

Ancient Rome.................................. 22

Centro Storico................................ 36

Tridente... 54

Trevi & the Quirinale.................... 66

Monti & Esquilino.......................... 80

San Giovanni & Celio 96

Aventino & Testaccio 108

Trastevere & Gianicolo................ 116

Vatican City & Prati...................... 130

Worth a Trip
San Lorenzo & Pigneto 78
Appian Way...92
Ostiense & San Paolo..............................106
Villa Borghese 146

Interior of the Basilica di Santa Maria Maggiore (p85)
IZZET KERIBAR/GETTY IMAGES ©

Explore

Ancient Rome

In a city of extraordinary beauty, Rome's ancient heart stands out. It's here that you'll find the great icons of the city's past: the Colosseum, the Palatino, the Roman and Imperial Forums, and Piazza del Campidoglio (pictured above), home to the mighty Capitoline Museums. Touristy by day, the area is quiet at night, with few after-hours attractions.

The Sights in a Day

Start early at the **Colosseum** (p24), Rome's fearsome gladiatorial arena. From there, continue on to the **Palatino** (p31) to see where Romulus supposedly founded the city. Before leaving the area take a moment to look down onto the **Roman Forum** (p26), your next destination. Once you've explored the ruins, exit the forum and climb up to **Piazza del Campidoglio** (p31) and the hilltop **Chiesa di Santa Maria in Aracoeli** (p31). Round the morning off with a doorstopper *panino* (sandwich) from **Alimentari Pannella Carmela** (p35).

After lunch, it's time for the **Capitoline Museums** (p31) and their collection of sculpture and major paintings. To clear your head afterwards, pop over to **Il Vittoriano** (p32) and take the lift to the top for Rome's best 360-degree views. If you've got energy for one last museum, the **Mercati di Traiano Museo dei Fori Imperiali** (p32) provides a thrilling overview of the Imperial Forums.

Finish the day with dinner at **Terre e Domus** (p33), a modern restaurant specialising in regional Lazio cuisine.

⊙ Top Sights

Colosseum (p24)

Roman Forum (p26)

💙 Best of Rome

History

Colosseum (p24)

Roman Forum (p26)

Palatino (p31)

Bocca della Verità (p33)

Architecture

Colosseum (p24)

Mercati di Traiano Museo dei Fori Imperiali (p32)

Piazza del Campidoglio (p31)

Getting There

Ⓜ **Metro** For the Colosseum, Forums and Palatino take metro line B to Colosseo.

🚌 **Bus** Many buses stop in or near Piazza Venezia, including buses 40, 64, 87, 170, 492, 916 and H.

Top Sights
Colosseum

Originally known as the Flavian Amphitheatre, the 50,000-seat Colosseum (Colosseo) is the most thrilling of Rome's ancient sights. It was here that gladiators met in mortal combat and where condemned prisoners fought wild beasts in front of baying, bloodthirsty crowds. Inaugurated in AD 80, it fell into disrepair after the fall of the Roman Empire, and was later used as a quarry for travertine and marble.

👁 Map p30, D4

www.coopculture.it

Piazza del Colosseo

adult/reduced incl Roman Forum & Palatino €12/7.50

🕣 8.30am-1hr before sunset

Ⓜ Colosseo

Interior of the Colosseum

Don't Miss

The Exterior

The outer walls, which were originally covered in travertine, have three levels of arches, framed by Ionic, Doric and Corinthian columns. The 80 entrance arches, known as *vomitoria,* allowed the spectators to enter and be seated in minutes, while up top, the upper level had supports for 240 masts that held up a canvas awning over the arena.

The Arena

The arena had a wooden floor covered in sand to prevent the combatants from slipping and to soak up the blood. It could also be flooded for mock sea battles. Trapdoors led down to the hypogeum, an underground complex of corridors, cages and lifts that served as the stadium's backstage area.

Seating

The *cavea,* for spectator seating, was divided into three tiers: magistrates and senior officials sat in the lowest tier, wealthy citizens in the middle and the plebs in the highest tier. Women (except for vestal virgins) were relegated to the cheapest sections at the top. The podium, a broad terrace in front of the tiers of seats, was reserved for emperors, senators and VIPs.

Arco di Costantino

Although not part of the Colosseum, the Arco di Costantino (Arch of Constantine) is a handsome landmark. Built in 312, it commemorates Constantine's victory over his rival Maxentius at the Battle of Ponte Milvio.

☑ **Top Tips**

▶ Visit in the early morning or late afternoon to avoid the crowds.

▶ If queues are long, buy your ticket at the Palatino (250m away at Via di San Gregorio 30).

▶ Other queue-jumping tips: get the Roma Pass; book your ticket at www.coopculture.it (plus a €2 booking fee); join an official English-language tour (€5 on top of the regular ticket).

▶ If you have your photo taken with a costumed centurion, they'll expect a tip – no more than €5.

▶ To visit the top tier and hypogeum you'll need to book a guided tour (€9).

✖ **Take a Break**

Avoid the rip-off food trucks outside the arena. Instead, search out Alimentari Pannella Carmela (p35) for a filling sandwich or head up to Cavour 313 (p35) for a light meal and glass of wine.

Top Sights
Roman Forum

The Roman Forum (Foro Romano) was ancient Rome's showpiece centre, a grandiose district of marble-clad temples, basilicas and vibrant public spaces. Its impressive, but badly labelled, ruins give some hint of this but you'll still have to use your imagination to picture it as it once was. The site was first developed in the 7th century BC when it was used as an Etruscan burial ground, but it fell into disrepair after the fall of the Roman Empire.

👁 Map p30, C3

www.coopculture.it

Largo della Salara Vecchia & Via Sacra

adult/reduced incl Colosseum & Palatino €12/7.50

🕑8.30am-1hr before sunset

🚇Via dei Fori Imperiali

View over the Roman Forum

Don't Miss

Via Sacra

Via Sacra, the Forum's main thoroughfare, connected the Palatino with the Roman Forum and Campidoglio. Lined with basilicas and temples – the **Basilica Fulvia Aemilia**, the **Tempio di Romolo**, the **Tempio di Antonino e Faustina** – it was part of the route that military commanders followed during the Roman Triumph, a ceremonial procession staged to honour their victories.

Tempio di Giulio Cesare

Little now remains of the Temple of Julius Caesar, aka the Tempio del Divo Giulio, erected by Augustus in 29 BC on the site where Caesar's body had been cremated 15 years earlier. Caesar was the first Roman to be posthumously deified, a custom that was central to the Roman imperial cult.

Curia

This big barnlike building was the official seat of the Roman Senate. Little remains of the 44 BC original and most of what you see today is a reconstruction of the Curia as it looked in the 3rd-century reign of Diocletian. In front, and hidden by scaffolding, is the **Lapis Niger**, a piece of black marble that's said to cover the tomb of Romulus.

Arco di Settimio Severo

One of the Roman Forum's signature monuments, and one of the finest examples of its type in Italy, the imposing 23m-high Arch of Septimius Severus was built in AD 203 to celebrate Roman victories over the Parthians. If you can make them out, reliefs in the central panel depict the defeated Parthians being led away in chains.

SAMMLER/GETTY IMAGES ©

☑ Top Tips

▶ Get grandstand views of the Roman Forum from the Palatino and Campidoglio.

▶ Visit early morning or late afternoon; crowds are worst between 11am and 2pm.

▶ It can get very hot and there's little shade, so take a hat and plenty of water.

▶ If you're caught short, there are toilets near the Chiesa di Santa Maria Antiqua.

✗ Take a Break

For a restorative coffee break head up to the Campidoglio and the Caffè Capitolino (p35). If you need something more substantial, search out Terre e Domus (p33), which serves traditional regional food.

Rostrum & Colonna di Foca

Near the Arco are the remains of the Rostrum, an elaborate podium where Shakespeare had Mark Antony make his famous 'Friends, Romans, countrymen...' speech and local politicos would harangue the crowds. Facing this, the Colonna di Foca (Column of Phocus), a free-standing, 13.5m-high column dating to AD 608, rises above what was once the Forum's main square, Piazza del Foro.

Tempio di Saturno

The eight granite columns that rise up behind the Colonna are all that remain of the Temple of Saturn, an important temple that doubled as the state treasury. Behind it (from north to south) are the ruins of the **Tempio della Concordia** (Temple of Concord), the **Tempio di Vespasiano** (Temple of Vespasian and Titus) and the **Portico degli Dei Consenti**.

Tempio di Castore e Polluce

Only three Corinthian columns remain of the Temple of Castor and Pollux, also known as the Tempio dei Castori. The temple, which dates to 489 BC, was dedicated to the Heavenly Twins after they supposedly led the Romans to victory over the Latin League in 496 BC.

Casa delle Vestali

White statues line the grassy atrium of the House of the Vestal Virgins, the once-luxurious, 50-room home of the virgins who tended the flame in the adjoining **Tempio di Vesta** (Temple of Vesta, goddess of hearth and household).

Basilica di Massenzio

Started by Emperor Maxentius and finished by Constantine (it's also known as the Basilica di Costantino) in 315, this vast basilica, the largest on the forum, covered an area of approximately 100m by 65m. In its original form the central hall was divided into enormous naves but only part of the northern nave has survived.

Arco di Tito

Said to be the inspiration for the Arc de Triomphe in Paris, the well-preserved Arch of Titus was built in AD 81 to celebrate Vespasian and Titus' victories against Jewish rebels in Jerusalem. In the past, Roman Jews would avoid passing under the arch, the historical symbol of the beginning of the Diaspora.

Understand ...
The Vestal Virgins

Despite privilege and public acclaim, life as a vestal virgin was no bed of roses. Every year six physically perfect patrician girls between the ages of six and 10 were chosen by lottery to serve in the Tempio di Vesta for a period of 30 years. If they lost their virginity they risked being buried alive and their lover being flogged to death.

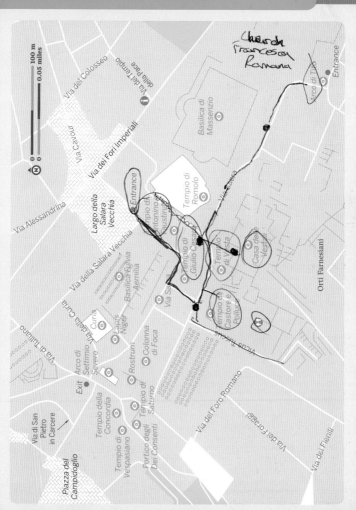

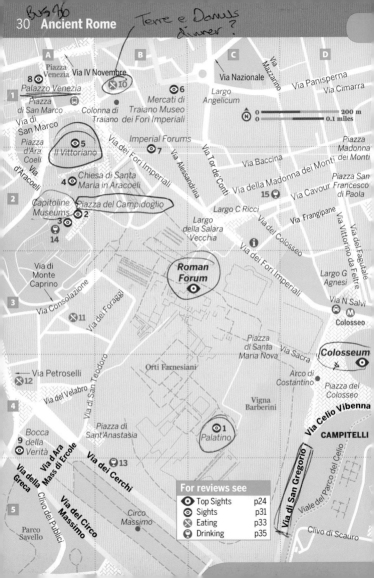

Bus 40

Terre e Danus dinner?

Map Labels

A
- Piazza Venezia
- Via IV Novembre
- 8 ⊙ Palazzo Venezia
- Piazza di San Marco
- ⊙ 10
- Via di San Marco
- Colonna di Traiano
- Piazza d'Ara Coeli
- ⊙ 5 Il Vittoriano
- Via d'Aracoeli
- 4 ⊙ Chiesa di Santa Maria in Aracoeli
- Capitoline Museums
- ⊙ 2 Piazza del Campidoglio
- 3 ⊙ 14
- Via di Monte Caprino
- Via Consolazione
- ⊗ 11 Via dei Foraggi
- Via Petroselli
- ⊗ 12
- Bocca della Verità 9 ⊙
- Via d'Ara Mass. di Ercole
- Via della Greca
- Via dei Cerchi
- ⊗ 13
- Clivo del Publici
- Via del Circo Massimo
- Parco Savello

B
- ⊙ 6 Mercati di Traiano Museo dei Fori Imperiali
- Imperial Forums
- ⊙ 7 Via dei Fori Imperiali
- Via Alessandrina
- Largo della Salara Vecchia
- Roman Forum ⊙
- Via di San Teodoro
- Orti Farnesiani
- Via del Velabro
- Piazza di Sant'Anastasia
- Palatino ⊙ 1
- Circo Massimo

C
- Via Mazzarino
- Via Nazionale
- Largo Angelicum
- Via Baccina
- Via della Madonna dei Monti
- 15 ⊙ Via Cavour
- Largo C Ricci
- Via del Colosseo
- ⊙ Via dei Fori Imperiali
- Piazza di Santa Maria Nova
- Via Sacra
- Arco di Costantino
- Piazza del Colosseo
- Vigna Barberini

D
- Via Panisperna
- Via Cimarra
- ⊙ 0 200 m
- 0 0.1 miles
- Piazza Madonna dei Monti
- Piazza San Francesco di Paola
- Via Frangipane
- Via Vittorino da Feltre
- Via del Fagutale
- Largo G Agnesi
- Via N Salvi
- ⊙ Colosseo
- **Colosseum** ⊙
- Via Celio Vibenna
- **CAMPITELLI**
- Via di San Gregorio
- Viale del Parco del Celio
- Clivo di Scauro

For reviews see	
⊙ Top Sights	p24
⊙ Sights	p31
⊗ Eating	p33
⊙ Drinking	p35

Sights

Tours – Roman Forum, Palatino, Colosseum

Palatino

ARCHAEOLOGICAL SITE

1 ⊙ Map p30, C4

Sandwiched between the Roman Forum and the Circo Massimo, the Palatino (Palatine Hill) is an atmospheric area of towering pine trees, majestic ruins and memorable views. It was here that Romulus supposedly founded the city in 753 BC and Rome's emperors lived in unabashed luxury. Look out for the **stadio** (stadium), the ruins of the **Domus Flavia** (Imperial Palace), and views over the Roman Forum from the **Orti Farnesiani**. (Palatine Hill; ☎06 3996 7700; www.coopculture.it; Via di San Gregorio 30 & Via Sacra; adult/reduced incl Colosseum & Roman Forum €12/7.50; ⊙8.30am–1hr before sunset; ⓂColosseo)

Piazza del Campidoglio

PIAZZA

2 ⊙ Map p30, A2

This hilltop piazza, designed by Michelangelo in 1538, is one of Rome's most beautiful squares. You can reach it from the Roman Forum, but the most dramatic approach is via the graceful **Cordonata** staircase up from Piazza d'Ara Coeli. The piazza is flanked by **Palazzo Nuovo** and **Palazzo dei Conservatori**, together home to the Capitoline Museums, and **Palazzo Senatorio**, seat of Rome city council. In the centre is a copy of an **equestrian statue** of Marcus Aurelius. (ⓆPiazza Venezia)

Capitoline Museums

MUSEUM

3 ⊙ Map p30, A2

Dating to 1471, the Capitoline Museums are the world's oldest public museums. Their collection of classical sculpture is one of Italy's finest, including crowd-pleasers such as the iconic *Lupa capitolina* (Capitoline Wolf), a sculpture of Romulus and Remus under a wolf, and the *Galata morente* (Dying Gaul), a moving depiction of a dying Gaul warrior. There's also a formidable picture gallery with masterpieces by the likes of Titian, Tintoretto, Rubens and Caravaggio. Note that ticket prices go up when there's a temporary exhibition on. (Musei Capitolini; ☎06 06 08; www.museicapitolini.org; Piazza del Campidoglio 1; adult/reduced €11.50/9.50; ⊙9.30am–7.30pm, last admission 6.30pm; ⓆPiazza Venezia)

Chiesa di Santa Maria in Aracoeli

CHURCH

4 ⊙ Map p30, A2

Atop the steep 14th-century Aracoeli staircase, this 6th-century Romanesque church marks the highest point of the Campidoglio. Its rich interior boasts several treasures including a wooden gilt ceiling, an impressive Cosmatesque floor and a series of 15th-century Pinturicchio frescoes illustrating the life of St Bernardine of Siena. Its main claim to fame, though, is a wooden baby Jesus that's thought to have healing powers. (Piazza Santa Maria in Aracoeli; ⊙9am–6.30pm summer, to 5.30pm winter; ⓆPiazza Venezia)

* coffee/lunch outside colosseum – on the hill, orange building

Il Vittoriano MONUMENT

5 ⊙ Map p30, A1

Love it or loathe it, as most locals do, you can't ignore Il Vittoriano (aka the Altare della Patria; Altar of the Fatherland), the massive mountain of white marble that towers over Piazza Venezia. Begun in 1885 to honour Italy's first king, Victor Emmanuel II, it incorporates the **Museo Centrale del Risorgimento** (www.risorgimento.it; adult/reduced €5/2.50; ⊘9.30am-6.30pm, closed 1st Mon of month), a small museum documenting Italian unification, and the **Tomb of the Unknown Soldier**.

> ## Understand
> ## Romulus & Remus
>
> According to legend, Romulus and Remus were the children of vestal virgin Rhea Silva and Mars, the god of war. While still babies, they were set adrift on the Tiber to escape their great-uncle Amulius, who was battling with their grandfather, Numitor, for control of Alba Longa. However, they were discovered by a she-wolf, who suckled them until a shepherd found and raised them.
>
> When Amulius later captured Remus, Romulus set him free, knocking off the king and paving the way for a city of their own. But the brotherly goodwill was short-lived: bickering over the new city walls drove Romulus to murder his brother and take full credit for the founding of Rome on 21 April 753 BC.

For Rome's best 360-degree views, take the **Roma dal Cielo** (adult/reduced €7/3.50; ⊘9.30am-6.30pm Mon-Thu, to 7.30pm Fri-Sun) lift to the top. (Piazza Venezia; admission free; ⊘9.30am-5.30pm summer, to 4.30pm winter; ☐Piazza Venezia)

Mercati di Traiano Museo dei Fori Imperiali MUSEUM

6 ⊙ Map p30, B1

This striking museum brings to life the **Mercati di Traiano**, emperor Trajan's great 2nd-century market complex, while also providing an introduction to the Imperial Forums with multimedia displays, explanatory panels and a smattering of artefacts. (✆06 06 08; www.mercatiditraiano.it; Via IV Novembre 94; adult/reduced €11.50/9.50; ⊘9.30am-7.30pm, last admission 6.30pm; ☐Via IV Novembre)

Imperial Forums ARCHAEOLOGICAL SITE

7 ⊙ Map p30, B2

The forums of Trajan, Augustus, Nerva and Caesar are known collectively as the Imperial Forums. These were largely buried when Mussolini bulldozed Via dei Fori Imperiali through the area in 1933, but excavations have since unearthed much of them. The standout sights are the **Mercati di Traiano** (Trajan's Markets), accessible through the Museo dei Fori Imperiali, and the landmark **Colonna di Traiano** (Trajan's Column). (Via dei Fori Imperiali; ☐Via dei Fori Imperiali)

Palazzo Venezia

PALACE

8 Map p30, A1

Built between 1455 and 1464, this was the first of Rome's great Renaissance palaces. For centuries it served as the embassy of the Venetian Republic, but it's most readily associated with Mussolini, who famously made speeches from the balcony. Nowadays, it's home to the tranquil **Museo Nazionale del Palazzo Venezia** (📞06 678 01 31; http://museopalazzovenezia.beniculturali.it; Via del Plebiscito 118; adult/reduced €5/2.50; ⏱8.30am-7.30pm Tue-Sun; 🚇Piazza Venezia) and its eclectic collection of Byzantine and early Renaissance paintings, furniture, bronze figures, weaponry and armour. (Piazza Venezia; 🚇Piazza Venezia)

Bocca della Verità

MONUMENT

9 Map p30, A4

A bearded face carved into a giant marble disc, the *Bocca della Verità* is one of Rome's most popular curiosities. Legend has it that if you put your hand in the mouth and tell a lie, the Bocca will slam shut and bite your hand off. The mouth, which was originally part of a fountain, or possibly an ancient manhole cover, now lives in the portico of the **Chiesa di Santa Maria in Cosmedin**, a handsome medieval church. (Mouth of Truth; Piazza Bocca della Verità 18; donation €0.50; ⏱9.30am-5.50pm summer, to 4.50pm winter; 🚇Piazza Bocca della Verità)

Detail of the Colonna di Traiano (Trajan's Column)

Eating

Terre e Domus

LAZIO CUISINE €€

10 Map p30, B1

This modern white-and-glass restaurant is the best option in the touristy Forum area. Overlooking the Colonna di Traiano, it serves a menu of traditional staples, all made with ingredients sourced from the surrounding Lazio region, and a selection of regional wines. Lunchtime can be busy but it quietens down in the evening. (📞06 6994 0273; Via Foro Traiano 82-4; meals €30; ⏱7.30am-12.30am Mon-Sat; 🚇Via dei Fori Imperiali)

Understand

Ancient Rome – a History

Rome started life as an amalgamation of Etruscan, Latin and Sabine settlements on the Palatino, Esquilino and Quirinale hills. It was initially ruled by Sabine and Etruscan kings but the death of Tarquinius the Proud paved the way for the birth of the Roman Republic in 509 BC.

The Republic

Under the Republic, Rome grew to become the Western world's undisputed superpower. Its armies conquered the Etruscans to the north and the Greeks and Carthaginians in the south. At home, it adopted a quasi-democratic system of government, based on a Senate and People's Assemblies – hence SPQR (Senatus Populusque Romanus, or the Senate and People of Rome). Roads were laid, including Via Appia Antica (Appian Way), a port was established at Ostia, and a sophisticated network of aqueducts and underground sewers was built.

The Roman Empire

By the 1st century BC the Republic was in trouble and when Julius Caesar was assassinated in 44 BC it finally collapsed, giving rise to a vicious power struggle. Octavian emerged victorious and in 27 BC became Rome's first emperor, Augustus. An enlightened ruler, he oversaw a period of peace and artistic development. But disaster was never far away and in AD 64 the city was devastated by a week-long fire. Nero blamed the Christians and executed many, including St Peter and St Paul. Yet the empire continued to flourish, and in about AD 100 it reached its zenith, stretching from Britannia to North Africa, and from Hispania to Syria.

Decline set in during the 3rd century. Barbarian invasions led Aurelian to build city walls and economic problems forced Diocletian to split the empire into eastern and western halves. Rivalries between the two empires culminated in the Battle of Milvian Bridge (312) and the accession of Constantine to the western throne. Constantine legalised Christianity before transferring to Byzantium (Istanbul) in 330, thus setting Rome on the route to ruin, which finally came in 476.

Alimentari Pannella Carmela

SANDWICHES €

11 Map p30, A3

A small, workaday food store concealed behind a curtain of creeping ivy, this is a lunchtime favourite supplying many local workers with fresh, cheap *panini* (sandwiches), pizza slices, salads and marinated vegetables. (Via dei Fienili 61; panini €2-3.50; ⏲8.30am-2.30pm Mon-Sat & 5-8pm Mon-Fri; 🚇Via Petroselli)

Ristorante Roof Garden Circus

RISTORANTE €€€

12 Map p30, A4

The rooftop of the Forty Seven hotel sets the romantic stage for chef Vito Grippa's menu of classic Roman dishes and contemporary Italian cuisine. With the Aventino hill rising in the background, you can tuck into stalwarts such as spaghetti *ajo e ojio* (with garlic and olive oil) or push the boat out and opt for something richer such as roast guinea fowl with black truffles. (📞06 678 78 16; www.fortysevenhotel.com; Hotel Forty Seven, Via Petroselli 47; meals €50; ⏲12.30-3pm & 7.30-11.30pm; 🚇Via Petroselli)

Drinking

0,75

BAR

13 🍺 Map p30, B5

This welcoming bar on the Circo Massimo is good for a lingering drink, an *aperitivo* (bar buffet; 6.30pm onwards) or a light meal (mains €6 to €13.50, salads €5.50 to €7.50). It's a friendly place with a laid-back vibe, an exposed-brick look and cool tunes. (www.075roma.com; Via dei Cerchi 65; ⏲11am-2am; 🛜; 🚇Via dei Cerchi)

Caffè Capitolino

CAFE

14 🍺 Map p30, A2

The Capitoline Museums' charming terrace cafe is a good place to relax over a drink or light snack (*panini, salads and pizza*) and enjoy wonderful views across the city's rooftops. Although part of the museum complex, you don't need a ticket to come here as it's accessible via an independent entrance on Piazzale Caffarelli. (Piazzale Caffarelli 4; ⏲9am-7.30pm Tue-Sun; 🚇Piazza Venezia)

Cavour 313

WINE BAR

15 🍺 Map p30, C2

Close to the Forum, wood-panelled Cavour 313 attracts everyone from tourists to actors and politicians. It serves a daily food menu and a selection of salads, cold cuts and cheeses (€8 to €12), but the headline act is the wine. And with more than 1200 labels to choose from you're sure to find something to tickle your palate. (📞06 678 54 96; www.cavour313.it; Via Cavour 313; ⏲12.30-2.45pm & 7.30pm-12.30am, closed Sun summer; Ⓜ Cavour)

Explore

Centro Storico

A tightly packed tangle of baroque piazzas, frescoed *palazzi* (mansions), cobbled alleyways, cafes and stylish bars, the historic centre is the Rome you're most likely pining for. The Pantheon and Piazza Navona (pictured above) are the star turns, but you'll also find a host of monuments, museums and churches, many with works by the likes of Michelangelo, Caravaggio, Bernini et al.

The Sights in a Day

☼ Kick-start your day with a coffee at **La Casa del Caffè Tazza d'Oro** (p50) before hitting the **Pantheon** (p38) early to avoid the crowds. Next, nip down to the **Basilica di Santa Maria Sopra Minerva** (p45) to glimpse a minor Michelangelo before heading via the **Chiesa di Sant'Ignazio di Loyola** (p45) to the **Galleria Doria Pamphilj** (p44) and its superb collection of Old Masters. That done, double back to **Armando al Pantheon** (p47) for an authentic Roman lunch.

☼ Recharged, push on to **Piazza Navona** (p44), Rome's showpiece baroque square. Nearby, the **Museo Nazionale Romano: Palazzo Altemps** (p44) houses some wonderful classical sculpture and the **Chiesa di San Luigi dei Francesi** (p44) boasts a trio of Caravaggios. To round off the day's sightseeing cross Corso Vittorio Emanuele II to check out **Campo de' Fiori** (p46) and **Palazzo Farnese** (p46).

☾ Spend the evening exploring the centre's animated backstreets. Dine on modern Italian fare at **Casa Coppelle** (p47), then join the cool crowd at **Barnum Cafe** (p50) or the neighbourhood gossips at **Caffè Sant'Eustachio** (p50).

For a local's day in the Centro Storico, see p40.

◉ **Top Sights**

Pantheon (p38)

◯ **Local Life**

A Day Out in the Centro Storico (p40)

♥ **Best of Rome**

Eating

Armando al Pantheon (p47)

Forno Roscioli (p49)

Supplizio (p47)

Venchi (p49)

Bars & Nightlife

Barnum Cafe (p50)

Caffè Sant'Eustachio (p50)

Getting There

🚌 **Bus** The best way to access the area. From Termini, buses 40 and 64 stop at Largo di Torre Argentina and continue down Corso Vittorio Emanuele II.

Ⓜ **Metro** There are no metro stations in the neighbourhood but it's within walking distance of Barberini, Spagna and Flaminio stations, all on line A.

🚊 **Tram** No 8 connects Via Arenula with Trastevere.

Top Sights
Pantheon

A striking 2000-year-old temple, now church, the Pantheon is Rome's best-preserved ancient monument and one of the most influential buildings in the Western world. Built by Hadrian over Marcus Agrippa's earlier temple, it has stood since AD 120, and although its greying, pockmarked exterior might look its age, inside it's a different story, and it remains a unique and exhilarating experience to pass through its vast bronze doors and gaze up at the largest unreinforced concrete dome ever built.

👁 Map p42, C3

Piazza della Rotonda

admission free

🕐 8.30am-7.30pm Mon-Sat, 9am-6pm Sun

🚃 Largo di Torre Argentina

Dome of the Pantheon

Don't Miss

The Exterior
Showing signs of wear, the monumental entrance portico is made up of 16 13m-high columns supporting a pediment. Little remains of the original decor but holes indicate where marble-veneer panels were once placed. The two 20-tonne bronze doors are 16th-century restorations of the originals.

The Inscription
For centuries the inscription under the pediment led historians to believe that the current temple was Marcus Agrippa's original. The wording suggests so, reading: 'M.AGRIPPA.L.F.COS.TER-TIUM.FECIT' or 'Marcus Agrippa, son of Lucius, consul for the third time, built this'. However, 19th-century excavations revealed traces of an earlier temple and scholars realised that Hadrian had simply kept Agrippa's original inscription.

The Interior
With light streaming in through the oculus (the hole in the centre of the dome), the marble-clad interior seems vast. Opposite the entrance is the main altar, while to the left are the tombs of artist Raphael, King Umberto I and Margherita of Savoy. On the opposite side of the rotunda is the tomb of King Vittorio Emanuele II.

The Dome
The Pantheon's dome, considered the Romans' most important architectural achievement, is the largest unreinforced concrete dome ever built. Its harmonious appearance is due to a precisely calibrated symmetry – the diameter is exactly equal to the building's interior height of 43.3m. Light (and rain) enters through the 8.7m-diameter oculus, which serves to absorb and redistribute the dome's huge tensile forces.

☑ **Top Tips**

▶ The Pantheon is a working church and mass is celebrated at 5pm on Saturdays and 10.30am on Sundays.

▶ Visit around midday to see a beam of light stream in through the oculus.

▶ Look down as well as up – the sloping marble floor has 22 almost-invisible holes to drain away rain that gets in through the oculus.

▶ Return after dark for amazing views of the building set against the ink-blue night sky

✖ **Take a Break**

The streets around the Pantheon are thick with eateries, cafes and bars. For an uplifting espresso, try La Casa del Caffè Tazza d'Oro (p50), one of the city's best coffee houses. For a quick gelato fix, make a beeline for Venchi (p49).

Local Life
A Day Out in the Centro Storico

Rome's historic centre casts a powerful spell. But it's not just visitors who fall for its romantic piazzas, suggestive lanes, and streetside cafes. Away from the tourist spotlight, locals love to spend time here, shopping, unwinding over a drink, taking in an exhibition or simply hanging out with friends.

① An Exhibition at the Chiostro del Bramante

Tucked away in the backstreets near Piazza Navona, the Renaissance **Chiostro del Bramante** (www.chiostrodelbramante.it; Via Arco della Pace 5; exhibitions adult/reduced €13/11; ☉church 9am-11.50pm Mon, Wed & Sat, cloister 10am-8pm; ☒Corso del Rinascimento) is a stunning setting for modern-art exhibitions. Afterwards, pop upstairs for a coffee, light lunch or drink at the smart in-house cafe.

Supplizo - snack food

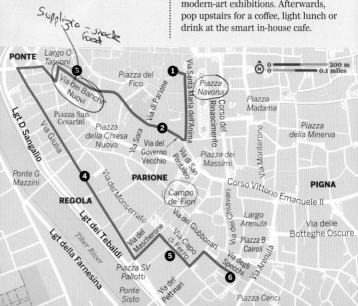

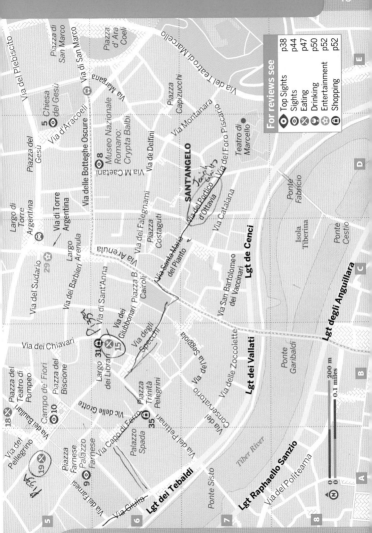

For reviews see

- Top Sights — p38
- Sights — p44
- Eating — p47
- Drinking — p50
- Entertainment — p52
- Shopping — p52

Piazza di San Marco

Piazza d'Ara Coeli

Via del Plebiscito

Via di San Marco

Via del Teatro di Marcello

Piazza del Gesù

Chiesa del Gesù

Via d'Aracoeli

Via della Botteghe Oscure

Piazza Capizucchi

Via Margana

Via Montanara

Museo Nazionale Romano: Crypta Balbi

Via de Delfini

Via M Caetani

SANT'ANGELO

Largo di Torre Argentina

Via di Torre Argentina

Via del Foro Piscario

Teatro di Marcello

Via del Portico d'Ottavia

Via Santa Maria del Pianto

Largo Arenula

Via Arenula

Via dei Falegnami

Piazza Costaguti

Via Catalana

Ponte Fabricio

Via del Sudario

Via dei Barbieri

Via dei Barbieri Arenula

Via di Sant'Anna

Via San Bartolomeo dei Vaccinari

Lgt de Cenci

Isola Tiberina

Ponte Cestio

Via del Chiavari

Via dei Giubbonari

Piazza B Cairoli

Via degli Specchi

Lgt degli Anguillara

Piazza del Teatro di Pompeo

Campo de' Fiori

Piazza del Biscione

Largo dei Librari

Via delle Grotte

Via della Seggiola

Via delle Zoccolette

Lgt dei Vallati

Ponte Garibaldi

Via dei Baullari

Via dei Baullari

Piazza Trinità Pellegrini

Via del Pettinari

Via del Conservatorio

Lgt dei Tebaldi

Via del Pellegrino

Piazza Farnese

Palazzo Farnese

Palazzo Spada

Via Capo di Ferro

Tiber River

Ponte Sisto

Via dei Farnesi

Via Giulia

Lgt Raphaello Sanzio

Via del Politeama

0.1 miles
200 m

N

Sights

Piazza Navona
PIAZZA

1 ◉ Map p42, B3

With its ornate fountains, baroque *palazzi* (mansions) and colourful cast of street artists, hawkers and tourists, Piazza Navona is central Rome's showcase square. Built over the 1st-century **Stadio di Domiziano** (Domitian's Stadium; ☎ 06 4568 6100; www.stadiodomiziano.com; Via di Tor Sanguigna 3; adult/reduced €8/6; ◷10am-7pm Sun-Fri, to 8pm Sat; ☐ Corso del Rinascimento), it was paved over in the 15th century and for almost 300 years hosted the city's main market. Its grand centrepiece is Bernini's **Fontana dei Quattro Fiumi** (Fountain of the Four Rivers; Piazza Navona; ☐ Corso del Rinascimento), featuring personifications of the rivers Nile, Ganges, Danube and Plate. (☐ Corso del Rinascimento)

Galleria Doria Pamphilj
MUSEUM

2 ◉ Map p42, E4

Hidden behind the grimy grey exterior of Palazzo Doria Pamphilj, this wonderful gallery boasts works by Raphael, Tintoretto, Brueghel, Titian, Caravaggio, Bernini and Velázquez. Masterpieces abound, but the star is Velázquez' portrait of an implacable Pope Innocent X, who grumbled that the depiction was 'too real'. For a comparison, check out Gian Lorenzo Bernini's sculptural interpretation of the same subject. (☎ 06 679 73 23; www.dopart.it; Via del Corso 305; adult/reduced €11/7.50; ◷9am-7pm, last admission 6pm; ☐ Via del Corso)

Museo Nazionale Romano: Palazzo Altemps
MUSEUM

3 ◉ Map p42, B2

Just north of Piazza Navona, Palazzo Altemps is a beautiful late-15th-century *palazzo*, housing the best of the Museo Nazionale Romano's collection of classical sculpture. Many pieces come from the celebrated Ludovisi collection, amassed by Cardinal Ludovico Ludovisi in the 17th century. (☎ 06 3996 7700; www.coopculture.it; Piazza Sant'Apollinare 44; adult/reduced €7/3.50; ◷9am-7.45pm Tue-Sun; ☐ Corso del Rinascimento)

Chiesa di San Luigi dei Francesi
CHURCH

4 ◉ Map p42, C3

Church to Rome's French community since 1589, this opulent baroque *chiesa* is home to a celebrated trio of Caravaggio paintings: the *Vocazione di San Matteo* (The Calling of Saint Matthew), the *Martiro di San Matteo* (The Martyrdom of Saint Matthew) and *San Matteo e l'angelo* (Saint Matthew and the Angel), known collectively as the St Matthew cycle. (Piazza di San Luigi dei Francesi 5; ◷10am-12.30pm & 3-7pm, closed Thu afternoon; ☐ Corso del Rinascimento)

Chiesa del Gesù
CHURCH

5 ◉ Map p42, D5

Rome's most important Jesuit church is a treasure trove of baroque art. Headline works include a swirling vault fresco by Giovanni Battista Gaulli (aka Il Baciccia), and Andrea del Pozzo's

GONZALO AZUMENDI/GETTY IMAGES ©

Sculpture at the Museo Nazionale Romano: Palazzo Altemps

opulent tomb for Ignatius Loyola. The Spanish saint lived in the church from 1544 until his death in 1556 and you can visit his **private rooms** to the right of the main building. (www.chiesadel gesu.org; Piazza del Gesù; ☉7am-12.30pm & 4-7.45pm, St Ignatius rooms 4-6pm Mon-Sat, 10am-noon Sun; ☐Largo di Torre Argentina)

Basilica di Santa Maria Sopra Minerva
BASILICA

6 ☉ Map p42, D4

Built on the site of three pagan temples, including one to the goddess Minerva, the Dominican Basilica di Santa Maria Sopra Minerva is Rome's only Gothic church. However, little remains of the original 13th-century structure

and these days the main drawcard is a minor Michelangelo sculpture and the colourful, art-rich interior. (www. santamariasopraminerva.it; Piazza della Minerva 42; ☉6.45am-7pm Mon-Fri, 6.45am-12.30pm & 3.30-7pm Sat, 8am-12.30pm & 3.30-7pm Sun; ☐Largo di Torre Argentina)

Chiesa di Sant'Ignazio di Loyola
CHURCH

7 ☉ Map p42, E3

Flanking a delightful rococo piazza, this important Jesuit church boasts a Carlo Maderno facade and two celebrated trompe l'oeil frescoes by Andrea Pozzo (1642–1709). One cleverly depicts a fake dome, whilst the other shows St Ignatius Loyola

Local Life
Jewish Ghetto

Centred on lively Via del Portico d'Ottavia, the **Jewish Ghetto** (Map p42, D7; 🚊 Lungotevere de' Cenci) is an atmospheric area studded with artisans studios, vintage-clothes shops, kosher bakeries and popular trattorias. Highlights include the **Area Archeologica del Teatro di Marcello e del Portico D'Ottavia** (entrances Via del Teatro di Marcello 44 & Via Portico d'Ottavia 29; admission free; ⏰ 9am-7pm summer, 9am-6pm winter; 🚊 Via del Teatro di Marcello) and its Colosseum-clone, Teatro di Marcello, and the **Museo Ebraico di Roma** (Jewish Museum of Rome; 🕿 06 6840 0661; www.museoebraico.roma.it; Via Catalana; adult/reduced €11/8; ⏰ 10am-6.15pm Sun-Thu, 9am-3.15pm Fri summer, 10am-4.15pm Sun-Thu, 9am-1.15pm Fri winter; 🚊 Lungotevere de' Cenci), which chronicles the city's Jewish history. Nearby, the **Isola Tiberina** is one of the world's smallest inhabited islands.

being welcomed into paradise. (Piazza di Sant'Ignazio; ⏰ 7.30am-7pm Mon-Sat, 9am-7pm Sun; 🚊 Via del Corso)

Museo Nazionale Romano: Crypta Balbi
MUSEUM

8 💿 Map p42, D6

The least known of the Museo Nazionale Romano's four museums, the Crypta Balbi sits over the ruins of several medieval buildings, themselves set atop the Teatro di Balbo (13 BC). Archaeological finds illustrate the urban development of the surrounding area, while the museum's underground excavations, visited by guided tour, provide an interesting insight into Rome's multilayered past. (🕿 06 3996 7700; www.coopculture.it; Via delle Botteghe Oscure 31; adult/reduced €7/3.50; ⏰ 9am-7.45pm Tue-Sun; 🚊 Via delle Botteghe Oscure)

Palazzo Farnese
HISTORIC BUILDING

9 💿 Map p42, A5

Home of the French embassy, this Renaissance *palazzo*, one of Rome's finest, was started in 1514 by Antonio da Sangallo the Younger, continued by Michelangelo and finished by Giacomo della Porta. Inside, it boasts a series of frecsoes by Annibale Carracci that are said by some to rival Michelangelo's in the Sistine Chapel. The highlight, painted between 1597 and 1608, is the monumental ceiling fresco *Amori degli Dei* (The Loves of the Gods) in the recently restored Galleria dei Carracci. (www.inventerrome.com; Piazza Farnese; admission €5; ⏰ guided tours 3pm, 4pm & 5pm Mon, Wed & Fri; 🚊 Corso Vittorio Emanuele II)

Campo de' Fiori
PIAZZA

10 💿 Map p42, B5

Noisy, colourful 'Il Campo' is a major focus of Roman life: by day it hosts one of Rome's best-known markets, while at night it morphs into a raucous open-air pub. For centuries the square was the site of public executions, and it was here that the philosopher Giordano Bruno was burned at the stake for heresy in 1600. The spot is marked by a sinister statue of the hooded monk, created by Ettore Ferrari and unveiled in 1889. (🚇Corso Vittorio Emanuele II)

Eating

Supplizio

FAST FOOD €

11 🍴 Map p42, A4

Rome's favourite snack, the *supplì* (a fried croquette filled with rice, tomato sauce and mozzarella), gets a gourmet makeover at this elegant new street-food joint. Sit back on the vintage leather sofa and dig into the classic article or throw the boat out and try something different, maybe some mildly spicy fish *supplì* stuffed with anchovies, tuna, parsley, and just a hint of orange. (Via dei Banchi Vecchi 143; supplì €3-5; ⏰noon-4pm Mon-Sat plus 5.30-10pm Mon-Thu, to 11pm Fri & Sat; 🚇Corso Vittorio Emanuele II)

Casa Coppelle

RISTORANTE €€

12 🍴 Map p42, C2

Exposed brick walls, flowers and sub-dued lighting set the stage for creative Italian- and French-inspired food at this intimate, romantic restaurant. There's a full range of starters and pastas, but the real tour de force are the deliciously tender steaks and rich meat dishes. Service is attentive and the setting, on a small piazza near the Pantheon, memorable. Book ahead. (☎06 6889 1707; www.casacoppelle.

it; Piazza delle Coppelle 49; meals €35-40; ⏰noon-3.30pm & 6.30-11.30pm; 🚇Corso del Rinascimento)

La Ciambella

ITALIAN €€

13 🍴 Map p42, C4

From breakfast pastries and lunch-time pastas to afternoon tea, Neapoli-tan pizzas and *aperitivo* (bar buffet) cocktails, this all-day eatery is a top find. Central but as yet undiscovered by the tourist hordes, it's a spacious, light-filled spot set over the ruins of the Terme di Agrippa, visible through transparent floor panels. The mostly traditional food is spot on, and the atmosphere laid back and friendly. (www.laciambellaroma.com; Via dell'Arco della Ciambella 20; fixed-price lunch menus €10-25, meals €30; ⏰7.30am-midnight; 🚇Largo di Torre Argentina)

Armando al Pantheon

TRATTORIA €€

14 🍴 Map p42, C3

An institution in these parts, Ar-mando al Pantheon is a rare find – a genuine family-run trattoria in the touristy Pantheon area. It's been on the go for more than 50 years and has served its fair share of celebs, but it hasn't let fame go to its head and it remains one of the best bets for earthy Roman cuisine. Reservations essential. (☎06 6880 3034; www.armandoalpantheon. it; Salita dei Crescenzi 31; meals €40; ⏰12.30-3pm & 7-11pm Mon-Fri, 12.30-3pm Sat; 🚇Largo di Torre Argentina)

Understand

Art & Architecture

In Rome you're constantly surrounded by great art and architecture. Walk around the centre and even without trying you'll stumble across masterpieces by the greats of the artistic pantheon.

The Renaissance

The Renaissance swept into Rome in the late 15th century, unleashing a massive overhaul of the medieval city. Leading the way was the architect Bramante, whose work on St Peter's Basilica was developed by Michelangelo, author of the basilica's dome and the spectacular frescoes in the Sistine Chapel. Artists, inspired by humanist philosophies, focused much energy on the depiction of the human form, resulting in two of the era's headline works: Michelangelo's *Pietà* in St Peter's Basilica and Raphael's *La scuola di Atene* (The School of Athens) in the Vatican Museums.

Baroque Flair

Emerging out of the Counter-Reformation, baroque art and architecture was dynamic, emotional and religiously inspired. Martyrdoms, ecstasies and miracles were depicted, and churches became increasingly ornamental. The key players were Gian Lorenzo Bernini, Francesco Borromini, and Caravaggio, whose lifelike portrayal of hitherto sacrosanct subjects caused uproar – such as his St Matthew cycle in the Chiesa di San Luigi dei Francesi. Bernini and Borromini were more mainstream in their approach – Bernini's sculptures in the Museo e Galleria Borghese and Borromini's Chiesa di San Carlo alle Quattro Fontane are definitive examples of their style.

Modern Times

The 20th century gave rise to two important movements: rationalism, a linear form of architecture that found full expression in the Esposizione Universale di Roma (Roman Universal Exhibition; EUR) area; and futurism, a modernist abstract style that you can explore at the Galleria Nazionale d'Arte Moderna e Contemporanea. More recently, a number of high-profile building projects have been completed in the city: Richard Meier's Museo dell'Ara Pacis, Renzo Piano's Auditorium Parco della Musica and Zaha Hadid's MAXXI.

Forno Roscioli
PIZZA, BAKERY €

15   Map p42, B6

This is one of Rome's top bakeries, much loved by lunching locals who crowd here for luscious sliced pizza, prize pastries and hunger-sating *supplì*. There's also a counter serving hot pastas and vegetable side dishes. (Via dei Chiavari 34; pizza slices from €2, snacks from €1.50; ☾7am-7.30pm Mon-Sat; ☐Via Arenula)

Venchi
GELATERIA €

16 Map p42, D3

Forget fancy flavours and gelato experiments, Venchi is all about the unadulterated enjoyment of chocolate. The wall shelves and counter displays feature myriad beautifully packaged delicacies, from pralines to chilli chocolate bars, as well as an assortment of decadent choc-based ice creams. (Via degli Orfani 87; gelato from €2.50; ☾10.30am-10pm Sun-Thu, to 11pm Fri & Sat; ☐Via del Corso)

Casa Bleve
RISTORANTE, WINE BAR €€€

17 Map p42, C4

Ideal for a special-occasion dinner, this palatial restaurant–wine bar dazzles with its column-lined dining hall and stained-glass roof. Its wine list, one of the best in town, accompanies a small but considered menu of hard-to-find cheeses, cold cuts, seasonal pastas and refined main courses. (☎06 686 59 70; www.casableve.it; Via del Teatro Valle 48-49; meals €50-65; ☾12.30-3pm & 7.30-10.30pm Mon-Sat; ☐Largo di Torre Argentina)

Ditirambo
ITALIAN €€

18 Map p42, B5

Since opening in 1996, Ditirambo has won an army of fans with its informal trattoria vibe and seasonal, organic cuisine. Dishes cover many bases, ranging from old-school favourites to thoughtful vegetarian offerings and more exotic fare such as pasta with Sicilian prawns, basil and lime. Book ahead. (☎06 687 16 26; www.ristoranteditirambo.it; Piazza della Cancelleria 72; meals €40; ☾1-3pm & 7.20-10.30pm, closed lunch Mon; ☐Corso Vittorio Emanuele II)

Forno di Campo de' Fiori
PIZZA, BAKERY €

19 Map p42, A5

This buzzing bakery on Campo de' Fiori does a roaring trade in *panini* (sandwiches) and delicious fresh-from-the-oven *pizza al taglio* (pizza by the slice). Aficionados swear by the *pizza bianca* ('white' pizza with olive oil, rosemary and salt), but the *panini* and *pizza rossa* ('red' pizza, with olive oil, tomato and oregano) taste plenty good, too. (Campo de' Fiori 22; pizza slices about €3; ☾7.30am-2.30pm & 4.45-8pm Mon-Sat; ☐Corso Vittorio Emanuele II)

Cul de Sac
WINE BAR, TRATTORIA €€

20 Map p42, B4

A perennially popular wine bar just off Piazza Navona, with an always-busy terrace and narrow, bottle-lined interior. Choose your tipple first – the wine list boasts about 1500 labels – and then pick what to go with it from the ample menu of no-nonsense Roman staples, Gallic-inspired cold cuts, pâtés and cheeses. Book ahead for the evening. (☎06 6880 1094; www.enotecaculdesacroma.it; Piazza Pasquino 73; meals €30; ⊙noon-12.30am; 🚊Corso Vittorio Emanuele II)

Drinking

Barnum Cafe
CAFE

21 Map p42, A4

A relaxed spot to check your email over a freshly squeezed orange juice or spend a pleasant hour reading a newspaper on one of the tatty armchairs in the white bare-brick interior. Come evening, the scene is cocktails, smooth tunes and coolly dressed-down locals. (www.barnumcafe.com; Via del Pellegrino 87; ⊙9am-10pm Mon, 8.30am-2am Tue-Sat; 🛜; 🚊Corso Vittorio Emanuele II)

Caffè Sant'Eustachio
CAFE

22 Map p42, C4

This small, unassuming cafe, generally three deep at the bar, is reckoned by many to serve the best coffee in town. Created by beating the first drops of espresso and several teaspoons of sugar into a frothy paste, then adding the rest of the coffee, it's guaranteed to put some zing into your sightseeing. (www.santeustachioilcaffe.it; Piazza Sant'Eustachio 82; ⊙8.30am-1am Sun-Thu, to 1.30am Fri, to 2am Sat; 🚊Corso del Rinascimento)

La Casa del Caffè Tazza d'Oro
CAFE

23 Map p42, D3

A busy, stand-up cafe with burnished 1940s fittings, this is one of Rome's best coffee houses. Its espresso hits the mark and there's a range of delicious coffee concoctions, including *granita di caffè,* a crushed-ice coffee drink served with whipped cream. There's also a small shop and, outside, a *bancomat* (coffee machine) for those out-of-hours caffeine emergencies. (www.tazzadorocoffeeshop.com; Via degli Orfani 84-86; ⊙7am-8pm Mon-Sat, 10.30am-7.30pm Sun; 🚊Via del Corso)

Etablì
BAR

24 Map p42, A3

Housed in a lofty 16th-century *palazzo,* Etablì is a rustic-chic lounge-bar-restaurant where you can drop by for a morning coffee, have a light lunch or chat over an *aperitivo.* It's laid-back and good-looking, with original French-inspired country decor – think leather armchairs, rough wooden tables, and a crackling fireplace. It also serves weekend brunch, restaurant dinners (€45), and hosts the occasional jam session. (☎06 9761 6694; www.etabli.it; Vicolo delle Vacche 9a; ⊙11am-2am, closed Mon in winter, Sun in summer; 🛜; 🚊Corso del Rinascimento)

Caffè Sant'Eustachio

No.Au
BAR

25 Map p42, A2

Opening onto a charming *centro storico* piazza, No.Au – pronounced Know How – is a cool bistro-bar set-up. Like many fashionable bars, it's big on beer and offers a knowledgeable list of artisanal craft brews, as well as local wines and a small but select food menu. (Piazza Montevecchio 16; ⏱6pm-1am Tue-Thu, noon-1am Fri-Sun; 🚇Corso del Rinascimento)

Il Goccetto
WINE BAR

26 Map p42, A4

This old-school *vino e olio* (wine and oil) shop has everything you could want in a neighbourhood wine bar – a colourful cast of regulars, a cosy, bottle-lined interior, a selection of cheeses and cold cuts, and a serious, 800-strong wine list. (Via dei Banchi Vecchi 14; ⏱11.30am-2pm Tue & Sat, 6.30pm-midnight Mon-Sat, closed Aug; 🚇Corso Vittorio Emanuele II)

Circus
BAR

27 Map p42, A3

A great little bar, tucked around the corner from Piazza Navona. It's a relaxed place popular with out-of-town students who come here to catch up on the news – wi-fi is free and there are international newspapers to read – and hang out over a drink. The atmosphere hots up in the evening when cocktails and shots take over from tea and cappuccino. (www.circus roma.it; Via della Vetrina 15; ⏰10.30am-2am; 📶; 🚇Corso del Rinascimento)

Salotto 42 BAR

28 Map p42, D2

On a picturesque piazza, facing the columns of the Temple of Hadrian, this is a glamorous lounge bar, complete with subdued lighting, vintage 1950s armchairs, Murano lamps and a collection of heavyweight design books. Come for the daily lunch buffet or to hang out with the 'see and be seen' crowd over an evening cocktail. (www.salotto42.it; Piazza di Pietra 42; ⏰10.30am-2am Tue-Sun; 🚇Via del Corso)

Entertainment

Teatro Argentina THEATRE

29 ⭐ Map p42, C5

Founded in 1732, Rome's top theatre is one of the two official homes of the Teatro di Roma – the other is the Teatro India in the southern suburbs. Rossini's *Barber of Seville* premiered here in 1816 and it today stages a wide-ranging program of drama (mostly in Italian), high-profile dance performances, and classical-music concerts. (📞06 6840 00311; www.teatrodiroma.net; Largo di Torre Argentina 52; tickets €16-29; 🚇Largo di Torre Argentina)

Shopping

Confetteria Moriondo & Gariglio FOOD

30 🔒 Map p42, D4

Roman poet Trilussa was so smitten with this historic chocolate shop – established by the Torinese confectioners to the royal house of Savoy – that he dedicated several sonnets to it. Many of the bonbons and handmade chocolates laid out in ceremonial splendour in the glass cabinets are still prepared according to original 19th-century recipes. (Via del Piè di Marmo 21-22; ⏰9am-7.30pm Mon-Sat; 🚇Via del Corso)

Ibiz – Artigianato in Cuoio ACCESSORIES

31 🔒 Map p42, B6

In their diminutive workshop, Elisa Nepi and her father craft exquisite leather goods, including wallets, bags, belts and sandals, in simple but classy designs and myriad colours. You can pick up a belt for about €35, while for a bag you should bank on at least €110. (Via dei Chiavari 39; ⏰9.30am-7.30pm Mon-Sat; 🚇Corso Vittorio Emanuele II)

Officina Profumo Farmaceutica di Santa Maria Novella BEAUTY

32 🔒 Map p42, B3

This, the Roman branch of one of Italy's oldest pharmacies, stocks natural perfumes and cosmetics as well as herbal infusions, teas and potpourri, all shelved in wooden, glass-fronted cabinets under a Murano chandelier. The original pharmacy was founded in Florence in 1612 by the Dominican monks of Santa Maria Novella, and many of its cosmetics are based on 17th-century herbal recipes. (www.sm novella.it; Corso del Rinascimento 47; ⊙10am-7.30pm Mon-Sat; ⊜Corso del Rinascimento)

Le Artigiane   CLOTHING, HANDICRAFTS

33 Map p42, C4

A space for local artisans to showcase their wares, this eclectic shop is the result of an ongoing project to sustain and promote Italy's artisanal traditions. It's a browser's dream with an eclectic range of handmade clothes, costume jewellery, ceramics, design objects and lamps. (www.leartigiane.it; Via di Torre Argentina 72; ⊙10am-7.30pm; ⊜Largo di Torre Argentina)

Nardecchia   ARTS

34 Map p42, B3

Famed for its antique prints, this historic Piazza Navona shop sells everything from 18th-century etchings by Giovanni Battista Piranesi to more affordable 19th-century panoramas. Bank on at least €150 for a small framed print. (Piazza Navona 25; ⊙10am-1pm Tue-Sat, 4.30-7.30pm Mon-Sat; ⊜Corso del Rinascimento)

Borini   SHOES

35 Map p42, B6

Don't be fooled by the discount, work-aday look – those in the know head to this seemingly down-at-heel shop for the latest footwear fashions. Women's styles, ranging from ballet flats to heeled boots, are displayed in the functional glass cabinets, alongside a small selection of men's leather shoes. (Via dei Pettinari 86-87; ⊙9am-1pm Tue-Sat, 3.30-7.30pm Mon-Sat; ⊜Via Arenula)

Bottega Pio La Torre   FOOD & DRINK

36 Map p42, C1

To look at it there's nothing special about Pio La Torre, a small, unpretentious food store near Piazza del Parlamento. But shop here and you're making a small but concrete contribution to the fight against the mafia. All the gastro goodies on sale, including organic olive oils, pastas, flours, honeys and wine, have been produced on land confiscated from organised crime outfits in Calabria and Sicily. (www.libera terra.it; Via dei Prefetti 23; ⊙10.30am-7.30pm Tue-Sat, 10.30am-2.30pm Sun, 3.30-7.30pm Mon; ⊜Via del Corso)

Luna & L'Altra   FASHION

37 Map p42, A4

An address for fashionistas with their fingers on the pulse, this is one of a number of independent boutiques on and around Via del Governo Vecchio. In its austere, gallery-like interior, clothes by Comme des Garçons, Issey Miyake, Yohji Yamamoto and others are exhibited in reverential style. (Piazza Pasquino 76; ⊙10am-2pm Tue-Sat, 3.30-7.30pm Mon-Sat; ⊜Corso Vittorio Emanuele II)

Explore

Tridente

Tridente is upscale and glamorous, full of designer boutiques, debonair bars and swish restaurants. Fashion pilgrims head to Via dei Condotti (pictured above) while tourists grab five on the Spanish Steps and people-watch on Piazza del Popolo, one of Rome's great piazzas. Art lovers can get their fill at the Renaissance Chiesa di Santa Maria del Popolo and modernist Museo dell'Ara Pacis.

The Sights in a Day

Breakfast at **Caffè Greco** (p64), the one-time refuge of Romantic poets, before heading up to **Piazza di Spagna** and the **Spanish Steps** (p56). Climb the staircase to the **Chiesa della Trinità dei Monti** (p57) where you're rewarded with wonderful rooftop views. Next, double back to search out **Via Margutta** (p59), the charming traffic-free street that Federico Fellini once called home. Follow on to **Piazza del Popolo** (p59) and the art-rich **Chiesa di Santa Maria del Popolo** (p59).

After lunch at **Al Gran Sasso** (p61), head to the **Museo dell'Ara Pacis** (p59) to admire ancient stonework in a cool, contemporary setting. Afterwards, indulge in some retail therapy, browsing the stores and boutiques on Via del Corso, **Via dei Condotti** (p60) and Via del Babuino.

Start the evening with an *aperitivo* (bar buffet) at **La Scena** (p63) before dinner at the **Enoteca Regionale Palatium** (p60). Round the day off by celeb-watching over cocktails at the **Stravinskij Bar – Hotel de Russie** (p63).

 Top Sights

Spanish Steps & Piazza di Spagna (p56)

Best of Rome

Eating

Imàgo (p61)

Enoteca Regionale Palatium (p60)

Fatamorgana (p60)

Dei Gracchi (p62)

Shopping

Fendi (p64)

Danielle (p64)

Pelletteria Nives (p65)

Getting There

Ⓜ Metro Get off at Spagna (line A) for Piazza di Spagna, the Spanish Steps, and Via dei Condotti, or at Flaminio (line A) for Piazza del Popolo.

🚌 Bus No 117 passes near to the Spanish Steps as it runs from Piazza del Popolo to Piazza di San Giovanni in Laterano.

Top Sights
Spanish Steps & Piazza di Spagna

Rising above Piazza di Spagna, the Spanish Steps are a favourite hang-out for footsore tourists, migrant hawkers and preening local teens. Posing has a long and noble history here and when Dickens visited in the 19th century he reported that artists' models would hang around in the hope of being hired for a painting. The area has long been a magnet to foreigners and in the late 1700s it was known as *er ghetto de l'inglesi* (the English ghetto).

◉ Map p58, D4

Piazza di Spagna

Ⓜ Spagna

View from the Spanish Steps to Piazza di Spagna

Don't Miss

The Steps

Although Piazza di Spagna was named after the nearby Spanish embassy to the Holy See, the monumental 135-step staircase (known in Italian as the Scalinata della Trinità dei Monti) was designed by an Italian, Francesco de Sanctis, and built in 1725 with money bequeathed by a French diplomat. At the top stands the Chiesa della Trinità dei Monti.

Chiesa della Trinità dei Monti

This landmark **church** (Map p58, D3; Piazza Trinità dei Monti; ⏲6.30am-8pm Tue-Sun; Ⓜ Spagna) was commissioned by King Louis XII of France and consecrated in 1585. Apart from the great rooftop views from outside, it boasts some wonderful frescoes by Daniele da Volterra. His *Deposizione* (Deposition), in the second chapel on the left, is regarded as a masterpiece of mannerist art.

Barcaccia

At the foot of the steps, the fountain of a sinking boat, the *Barcaccia* (1627), is believed to be by Pietro Bernini, father of the more famous Gian Lorenzo. It's fed from the ancient Acqua Vergine aqueduct, but there's not much water pressure, so the structure is cleverly sunk into the piazza. Bees and suns adorn the boat, symbols of the Barberini family who commissioned it.

Around the Piazza

Flanking the steps is the *palazzo* (mansion) where Romantic poet John Keats died in 1821. Opposite, **Via dei Condotti** is Rome's most exclusive shopping strip, while to the southeast, adjacent **Piazza Mignanelli** is dominated by the **Colonna dell'Immacolata**, built in 1857 to celebrate Pope Pius IX's declaration of the Immaculate Conception.

☑ Top Tips

▶ To catch the steps in full bloom, visit in late April or early May, when they're decorated with vases of brightly coloured azaleas.

▶ Steer clear of the piazza on Saturday afternoons, when it's full of adolescents on heat.

▶ If you don't fancy climbing the steps, take the lift from the entrance/exit of Spagna metro station.

▶ Officially, you're not allowed to eat on the steps.

✗ Take a Break

Duck out of the piazza and head to nearby Gina (p61) to leave the crowds behind and indulge in a stylish snack or light lunch. Alternatively, recharge your batteries with an *aperitivo* at the Enoteca Regionale Palatium (p60).

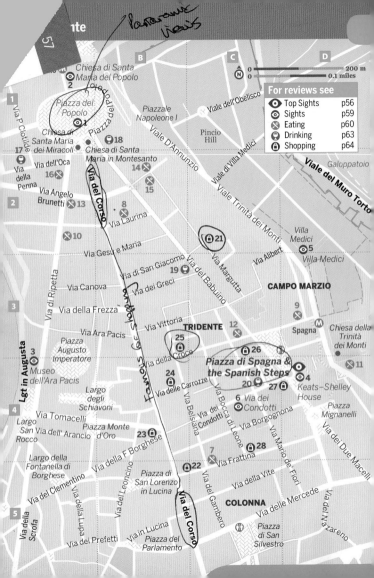

Sights

Piazza del Popolo
PIAZZA

1 ⊚ Map p58, A1

This dazzling piazza was laid out in 1538 to provide a grandiose entrance to what was then Rome's main northern gateway. It has since been remodelled several times, most recently by Giuseppe Valadier in 1823. Guarding its southern approach are Carlo Rainaldi's twin 17th-century churches, **Chiesa di Santa Maria dei Miracoli** and **Chiesa di Santa Maria in Montesanto**. In the centre, the 36m-high **obelisk** was brought by Augustus from ancient Egypt and originally stood in Circo Massimo. (Ⓜ Flaminio)

Chiesa di Santa Maria del Popolo
CHURCH

2 ⊚ Map p58, A1

A magnificent repository of art, this is one of Rome's earliest and richest Renaissance churches. Of the numerous works of art on display, it is the two Caravaggio masterpieces that draw the most onlookers – the *Conversion of Saul* and the *Crucifixion of St Peter* – but it contains other fine works, including several by Pinturicchio and Bernini. (Piazza del Popolo; ⊘7am-noon & 4-7pm Mon-Sat, 7.30am-1.30pm & 4.30-7.30pm Sun; Ⓜ Flaminio)

Q Local Life
Via Margutta

A narrow lane lined with art studios, antique shops and ochre *palazzi* (mansions), **Via Margutta** (Map 58, C3; Ⓜ Spagna) is picture-perfect Rome. It has long had an arty reputation and it was in the Valeria Moncada Gallery at No 54 that the futurists held their first meeting and Picasso met his wife Olga. More recently, Federico Fellini lived at No 110 until his death in 1993.

Museo dell'Ara Pacis
MUSEUM

3 ⊚ Map p58, A4

The first modern construction in Rome's historic centre since WWII, Richard Meier's controversial and widely detested glass-and-marble pavilion houses the *Ara Pacis Augustae* (Altar of Peace), Augustus' great monument to peace. One of the most important works of ancient Roman sculpture, the vast marble altar – measuring 11.6m by 10.6m by 3.6m – was completed in 13 BC. (⤶06 06 08; http://en.arapacis.it; Lungotevere in Auga; adult/reduced €10.50/8.50; ⊘9am-7pm, last admission 6pm; Ⓜ Flaminio)

Keats-Shelley House
MUSEUM

4 ⊚ Map p58, D4

The Keats-Shelley House is where Romantic poet John Keats died of tuberculosis at the age of 25, in

February 1821. A year later, fellow poet Percy Bysshe Shelley drowned off the coast of Tuscany. The small apartment evokes the impoverished lives of the poets, and is now a small museum crammed with memorabilia, from faded letters to death masks. (☎ 06 678 42 35; www.keats-shelley-house.org; Piazza di Spagna 26; adult/reduced €5/4, ticket gives discount for Casa di Goethe; ⏰ 10am-1pm & 2-6pm Mon-Fri, 11am-2pm & 3-6pm Sat; Ⓜ Spagna)

Villa Medici

PALACE

5 ◉ Map p58, D2

This sumptuous Renaissance palace was built for Cardinal Ricci da Montepulciano in 1540, but Ferdinando dei Medici bought it in 1576. It remained in Medici hands until 1801, when Napoleon acquired it for the French Academy. Take a tour to see the wonderful landscaped **gardens**, cardinal's **painted apartments**, and incredible **views** over Rome. Note the pieces of ancient Roman sculpture from the Ara Pacis embedded in the villa's walls. (☎ 06 6 76 11; www.villamedici.it; Viale Trinità dei Monti 1; gardens adult/reduced €12/6; ⏰ tours Tue-Sun in Italian, French & English, check website for current times; cafe 11am-6pm Tue-Sun; Ⓜ Spagna)

Via dei Condotti

AREA

6 ◉ Map p58, C4

High-rolling shoppers and window-dreamers take note, this is Rome's smartest shopping strip. At the eastern end, near Piazza di Spagna, Caffè

Greco (p64) was a favourite meeting point of 18th- and 19th-century writers. Other top shopping streets in the area include **Via Frattina, Via della Croce, Via delle Carrozze** and **Via del Babuino.** (Ⓜ Spagna)

Eating

Enoteca Regionale Palatium

RISTORANTE, WINE BAR €€€

7 Map p58, C4

A rich showcase of regional bounty, run by the Lazio Regional Food Authority, this sleek wine bar serves excellent local specialities, such as *porchetta* (pork roasted with herbs) or *gnocchi alla Romana con crema da zucca* (potato dumplings Roman-style with cream of pumpkin), as well as an impressive array of Lazio wines (try lesser-known drops such as Aleatico). *Aperitivo* is a good bet too. (☎ 06 692 02 132; Via Frattina 94; meals €55; ⏰ 11am-11pm Mon-Sat, closed Aug; 🚇 Via del Corso)

Fatamorgana

GELATERIA €

8 Map p58, B2

The wonderful all-natural Fatamorgana, purveyors of arguably Rome's best artisanal ice cream, now has this handy central branch. Innovative and classic tastes of heaven abound, including flavours such as pear and caramel, all made from the finest seasonal ingredients. (Via Laurina 10; ⏰ noon-11pm; Ⓜ Flaminio)

Understand
La Passeggiata

One of the quintessential rituals of Roman life is the daily *passeggiata* (promenade). Every evening, typically between 5pm and 8pm, locals of all ages pour onto the streets to hang out in the piazzas and parade along the main thoroughfares. In eras past the *passeggiata* was the time for officially sanctioned courting, and parents would encourage their eligible daughters to don their finest clothes and put on a good performance. Still today, Romans like to dress up and show their colours, particularly at weekends when families, friends and lovers take to the streets en masse. For the best spectacle, head to Via del Corso and the streets around Piazza di Spagna.

Gina   CAFE €

9 ⊗ Map p58, D3

Around the corner from the Spanish Steps, this is an ideal place to drop once you've shopped. Comfy white seats are strewn with powder-blue cushions, and it gets packed by a Prada-clad crowd, gossiping and flirting over sophisticated salads and perfect *panini* (sandwiches). You can also order a €40/60 regular/deluxe picnic-for-two to take up to Villa Borghese. (☎06 678 02 51; Via San Sebastianello 7a; snacks €8-16; ⊙11am-8pm; Ⓜ Spagna)

Al Gran Sasso   TRATTORIA €€

10 ⊗ Map p58, A2

A top lunchtime spot, this is a classic, dyed-in-the-wool trattoria specialising in old-school country cooking. It's a relaxed place with a welcoming vibe, garish murals on the walls (strangely often a good

sign) and tasty, value-for-money food. The fried dishes are excellent, or try one of the daily specials, chalked up on the board outside. (☎06 321 48 83; www.algransasso. com; Via di Ripetta 32; meals €35; ⊙12.30-2.30pm & 7.30-11.30pm Sun-Fri; Ⓜ Flaminio)

Imàgo   ITALIAN €€€

11 ⊗ Map p58, D4

Even in a city of great views, the panoramas from the Hassler Hotel's Michelin-starred romantic rooftop restaurant are special (request the corner table), extending over a sea of roofs to the great dome of St Peter's Basilica. Complementing the views are the bold, mod-Italian creations of culinary whizz, chef Francesco Apreda. Book ahead. (☎06 6993 4726; www.imagorestaurant.com; Piazza della Trinità dei Monti 6; tasting menus veg/meat €120/130-140; ⊙7-10.30pm; Ⓜ Spagna)

Casa Conti ITALIAN €€

12 Map p58, C3

This unique place has double-height ceilings and original tiled floors, and is filled by fascinating antiques. With few tables, it's a great hideaway for a simple Roman lunch with a simple dish of the day such as fettucine, and a wide choice of delicious wines. Delicious desserts may include *cannolo* (Sicilian tube pastry), *crostata* (jam tart), tiramisu or chocolate tart. (06 6920 0735; Via della Croce; meals €40; 1-3pm Mon-Sat; Spagna)

Buccone RISTORANTE, WINE BAR €

13 Map p58, A2

Step in under the faded gilt-and-mirrored sign and you'll feel as though you've gone back in time. Once a coach house, then a tavern, this building became Buccone in the 1960s, furnished with 19th-century antiques and lined with around a thousand Italian wines. It serves simple food such as mixed plates of cured meat and cheese, but on Saturday offers a proper hot *cena* (dinner). (06 361 21 54; Via di Ripetta 19; meals €20; 12.30-2.30pm & 7.30-10.30pm Mon-Sat; Flaminio)

Babette ITALIAN €€€

14 Map p58, B2

Babette is run by two sisters who used to produce a fashion magazine, which accounts for its effortlessly chic interior of exposed brick walls and vintage painted signs. You're in for a feast too, as the cooking is delicious, with a so-phisticated, creative French twist (think *tortiglioni* with courgette and pistachio pesto). The *torta Babette* is the food of the gods, a light-as-air lemon cheesecake. (06 321 15 59; Via Margutta 1; meals €45-55; 1-3pm Tue-Sun, 7-10.45pm daily, closed Jan & Aug; ; Spagna, Flaminio)

Il Margutta RistorArte VEGETARIAN €€

15 Map p58, B2

Vegetarian restaurants in Rome are rarer than parking spaces, and this airy art gallery–restaurant is an unusually chic way to eat your greens. Dishes are excellent and most produce is organic, with offerings such as artichoke hearts with potato cubes and smoked provolone cheese. Best value is the weekday (€15 to €18) and weekend (€25) buffet brunch. There's a vegan menu and live music weekends. (06 678 60 33; www.ilmargutta.it; Via Margutta 118; meals €40; 12.30-3pm & 7-11.30pm; ; Spagna, Flaminio)

Dei Gracchi GELATERIA €

16 Map p58, A2

A new outpost of the venerable Gelataria dei Gracchi, close to the Vatican, this serves up superb ice cream made from the best ingredients, with an excellent array of classic flavours. It's handily located just off Piazza del Popolo, so you can take your pick and then wander around the square as you revel in your excellent selection. (Via di Ripetta 261; gelato from €2; 11.30am-10pm, to midnight Jun-Sep; Flaminio)

Hotel de Russie

Drinking

La Scena

BAR

17 Map p58, A2

Part of the art-deco Hotel Locarno, this bar has a faded Agatha Christie–era feel, and a greenery-shaded outdoor terrace bedecked in wrought-iron furniture. Cocktails cost €13 to €15, or you can partake of afternoon tea from 3pm to 6pm and *aperitivo* from 7pm to 10pm. (Via della Penna 22; ⏰7am-1am; MFlaminio)

Stravinskij Bar – Hotel de Russie

BAR

18 Map p58, B1

Can't afford to stay at the celeb-magnet Hotel de Russie? Then splash out on a drink at its swish bar. There are sofas inside, but best is a drink in the sunny courtyard, with sunshaded tables overlooked by terraced gardens. Impossibly romantic in the best *dolce vita* style, it's perfect for a cocktail (from €20) or beer (€13) and some posh snacks. (☎06 328 88 70; Via del Babuino 9; ⏰9am-1am; MFlaminio)

...ni CAFE

📍p p58, B3

...8 sculptor Canova signed a contract for this studio that agreed it would be forever preserved for sculpture. The place is still stuffed with statues and it's a unique experience to sit among the great maquettes and sup an upmarket tea or knock back some wine and snacks. (📞 06 3211 0702; Via del Babuino 150a/b; ⏰9am-10.30pm Mon-Sat; Ⓜ Spagna)

Caffè Greco CAFE

20 🏺 Map p58, C4

Caffè Greco opened in 1760 and is still working the look: penguin waiters, red flock and age-spotted gilt mirrors. Casanova, Goethe, Wagner, Keats, Byron, Shelley and Baudelaire were all once regulars. Now there are fewer artists and lovers and more shoppers and tourists. Prices reflect this, un-

less you do as the locals do and have a drink at the bar (*caffè* bar/seated €1.50/6). (📞 06 679 17 00; Via dei Condotti 86; ⏰9am-9pm; Ⓜ Spagna)

Shopping

Bottega di Marmoraro ARTS

21 🔒 Map p58, C2

A particularly charismatic hole-in-the-wall shop lined with marble carvings, where you can get marble tablets engraved with any inscription you like (€15). Peer inside at lunchtime and you might see the cheerfully quizzical *marmoraro* (marble worker), Enrico Fiorentini, cooking pasta for his lunch next to the open log fire. (Via Margutta 53b; ⏰8am-7.30pm Mon-Sat; Ⓜ Flaminio)

Danielle SHOES

22 🔒 Map p58, B5

If you're female and in need of an Italian shoe fix, this is an essential stop on your itinerary. It sells both classic and fashionable styles – foxy heels, boots and ballet pumps – at extremely reasonable prices. Shoes are soft leather and come in myriad colours. (📞 06 679 24 67; Via Frattina 85a; ⏰10.30am-7.30pm; Ⓜ Spagna)

Fendi CLOTHING

23 🔒 Map p58, B4

A temple to subtly blinging accessories, this multistorey art-deco building is the Fendi mothership: this is the

---

Ⓠ Local Life

Pastificio

For most of the day, **Pastificio** (Map p58, C3; Via della Croce 8; pasta, wine & water €4; ⏰lunch 1-3pm Mon-Sat; Ⓜ Spagna) goes about its business as a fresh pasta shop but at lunchtime it turns itself into the neighbourhood's budget diner. Locals pile in to fill up on the daily pasta dishes (there's a choice of two), eaten out of plastic bowls wherever there's room.

global headquarters, as the brand was born in Rome. Fendi is particularly famous for its products made of leather and (more controversially) fur. (☎06 69 66 61; Largo Goldoni 420; ⊙10am-7.30pm Mon-Sat, 11am-2pm & 3-7pm Sun; ⓜSpagna)

Pelletteria Nives   ACCESSORIES

24 🔒 Map p58, B4

Take the rickety lift to this workshop, choose from the softest leathers, and you will shortly be the proud owner of a handmade, designer-style bag, wallet, belt or briefcase – take a design with you. Bags cost €200 to €350 and take around a week to make. (☎333 3370831; Via delle Carrozze 16; ⊙9am-1pm & 4-8pm Mon-Sat; ⓜSpagna)

Vertecchi Art   ARTS

25 🔒 Map p58, B3

Ideal for last-minute gift buying, this large paperware and art shop has beautiful printed paper, cards and envelopes that will inspire you to bring back the art of letter writing, plus an amazing choice of notebooks, art stuff and trinkets. (Via della Croce 70; ⊙3.30-7.30pm Mon, 10am-7.30pm Tue-Sat; ⓜSpagna)

C.U.C.I.N.A.   HOMEWARES

26 🔒 Map p58, C3

If you need a foodie gadget, C.U.C.I.N.A. is the place. Make your own *cucina* (kitchen) look the part

with the designerware from this famous shop, with myriad devices you'll decide you simply must have, from jelly moulds to garlic presses. (☎06 679 12 75; Via Mario de' Fiori 65; ⊙3.30-7.30pm Mon, 10am-7.30pm Tue-Fri, 10.30am-7.30pm Sat; ⓜSpagna)

Sermoneta   ACCESSORIES

27 🔒 Map p58, D4

Buying leather gloves in Rome is a rite of passage for some, and its most famous glove-seller is the place to do it. Choose from a kaleidoscopic range of quality leather and suede gloves lined with silk and cashmere. An expert assistant will size up your hand in a glance. Just don't expect them to crack a smile. (☎06 679 19 60; www.sermonetagloves.com; Piazza di Spagna 61; ⊙9.30am-8pm Mon-Sat, 10am-7pm Sun; ⓜSpagna)

Fausto Santini   SHOES

28 🔒 Map p58, C4

Rome's best-known shoe designer, Fausto Santini is famous for his beguilingly simple, architectural shoe designs, with beautiful boots and shoes made from butter-soft leather. Colours are beautiful, the quality impeccable. Seek out the end-of-line discount shop (p91) if this looks out of your price range. (☎06 678 41 14; Via Frattina 120; ⊙11am-7.30pm Mon, 10am-7.30pm Tue-Sat, 11am-2pm & 3-7pm Sun; ⓜSpagna)

Explore

Trevi & the Quirinale

Home to *that* fountain, Trevi's lively medieval streets feel a bit like a circus with their tourist hordes and tacky souvenir shops. But head up the Quirinale hill and the atmosphere changes as you come face to face with the presidential Palazzo del Quirinale and a number of distinguished baroque churches. Other hot spots include Palazzo Barberini and the Saturday-only Galleria Colonna.

The Sights in a Day

Start the day with an awe-inspiring Bernini masterpiece at the **Chiesa di Santa Maria della Vittoria** (p71). For a further fill of baroque pomp and Renaissance revelations head to the **Galleria Nazionale d'Arte Antica: Palazzo Barberini** (p71), a superb art gallery housed in one of Rome's great aristocratic *palazzi* (mansions). Next, lunch at **Colline Emiliane** (p74).

Fed and watered, head uphill to the Quirinale. Check out Borromini's **Chiesa di San Carlo alle Quattro Fontane** (p71) and push on to Piazza del Quirinale and the majestic **Palazzo del Quirinale** (p72). If there's an exhibition on, stop at the **Scuderie Papali al Quirinale** (p72), otherwise duck down the steps near the piazza and continue on to the **Trevi Fountain** (p68). Throw your coins into the water and then treat yourself to a gelato from **San Crispino** (p76).

Wind up the day with food and cocktails at **Baccano** (p75) and late-night jazz tunes at **Gregory's** (p77).

Top Sights

Trevi Fountain (p68)

Best of Rome

History

Trevi Fountain (p68)

Art

Santa Teresa trafitta dall'amore di Dio (Ecstasy of St Teresa), Chiesa di Santa Maria della Vittoria (p71)

Il Trionfo della Divina Provvidenza (Triumph of Divine Providence), Galleria Nazionale d'Arte Antica: Palazzo Barberini (p71)

Culture

Gregory's (p77)

Scuderie Papali al Quirinale (p72)

Architecture

Chiesa di San Carlo alle Quattro Fontane (p71)

Chiesa di Sant'Andrea al Quirinale (p72)

Getting There

M Metro Get off at Barberini (line A) for the Trevi Fountain, Quirinale and Via Vittorio Veneto.

Bus Take bus 40, 64 or H for Via Nazionale, from where you can access the Quirinale; buses 53 and 85 stop at Piazza Barberini, near the metro station.

Top Sights
Trevi Fountain

The Fontana di Trevi, immortalised by Anita Ek-berg's dip in *La Dolce Vita,* is Rome's largest and most famous fountain. A theatrical ensemble of mythical figures, wild horses and cascading rock falls, it takes up the entire side of 17th-century Palazzo Poli. The water is supplied by the Aqua Virgo, a 2000-year-old aqueduct that connects the capital with springs 19km away. Completed in 1762, it's named Trevi in reference to the *tre vie* (three roads) that converge on it.

👁 Map p70, A3

Piazza di Trevi

Ⓜ Barberini

A Triton leading a horse in the Trevi Fountain

Don't Miss

Neptune & His Seahorses

Designed by Nicola Salvi in 1732, the fountain depicts Neptune, the god of the sea, in a shell-shaped chariot being led by Tritons and two seahorses – one wild, one docile – representing the moods of the sea. In the niche to the left of Neptune, a statue represents Abundance; to the right is Salubrity.

Throwing in Your Coin

The famous tradition is to toss a coin into the water and thus ensure you'll one day return to Rome. About €3000 is thrown in on an average day. For years much of this was scooped up by local thieves but in 2012 the city authorities clamped down, making it illegal to remove coins from the water. The money is now collected daily and handed over to the Catholic charity Caritas.

Asso di Coppe

Look on the wall to the right of the fountain and you'll see a strange conical urn. This is the *Asso di coppe* (Ace of Cups) that Nicola Salvi placed there to block the view of a busybody barber who had criticised the fountain's design during its construction.

Trevi Fountain Films

The fountain has featured in a number of classic films. It set the stage for Anita Ekberg's splash in *La Dolce Vita* (1960) – apparently she wore waders under her iconic black dress – and appeared in *Roman Holiday* (1953) and *Three Coins in the Fountain,* a cheesy 1954 romance which popularised the coin-throwing tradition.

☑ Top Tips

▶ Avoid the crowds and come at the crack of dawn.

▶ Have some coins ready to throw in.

▶ Costumed centurions hang around the fountain volunteering to pose with you for your photos. They expect payment.

▶ The fountain's dazzling white stone photographs best in soft late-afternoon light.

▶ Come after dark to see the fountain magically illuminated.

✗ Take a Break

For a quick fuel stop or an easy takeaway lunch, search out Da Michele (p75) and grab a slice of pizza. For something more substantial, try for an outdoor table at the popular Tuscan wine bar–restaurant, Il Chianti (p75).

For reviews see

🔴	Top Sights	p68
🟢	Sights	p71
✖	Eating	p74
🟢	Drinking	p77
🟢	Entertainment	p77
🔵	Shopping	p77

400 m
0.2 miles

Sights

Chiesa di Santa Maria della Vittoria
CHURCH

1 ◉ Map p70, E2

This modest church is an unlikely setting for an extraordinary work of art – Bernini's extravagant and sexually charged *Santa Teresa trafitta dall'amore di Dio* (Ecstasy of St Teresa). This daring sculpture depicts Teresa, engulfed in the folds of a flowing cloak, floating in ecstasy on a cloud while a teasing angel pierces her repeatedly with a golden arrow. (Via XX Settembre 17; ⊘8.30am-noon & 3.30-6pm; Ⓜ Repubblica)

Galleria Nazionale d'Arte Antica: Palazzo Barberini
GALLERY

2 ◉ Map p70, C3

Commissioned to celebrate the Barberini family's rise to papal power, Palazzo Barberini is a sumptuous baroque palace that impresses even before you go inside and start on the breathtaking art. Many high-profile architects worked on it, including rivals Bernini and Borromini: the former contributed a large squared staircase, the latter a helicoidal one. (✆06 3 28 10; www.galleriabarberini. beniculturali.it; Via delle Quattro Fontane 13; adult/reduced €7/3.50, incl Palazzo Corsini, valid 3 days €9/4.50; ⊘8.30am-7pm Tue-Sun; Ⓜ Barberini)

Local Life
Sunsets on the Quirinale

One of the best places to catch a memorable Roman view is **Piazza del Quirinale** (Map p70, B4; Ⓜ Barberini) in front of the presidential palace. As the sun dips and the sky takes on a golden, fiery hue you can gaze over a sea of rooftops to the distant dome of St Peter's Basilica (Basilica di San Pietro).

Chiesa di San Carlo alle Quattro Fontane
CHURCH

3 ◉ Map p70, D3

This tiny church is a masterpiece of Roman baroque. It was Borromini's first church, and the play of convex and concave surfaces and the dome illuminated by hidden windows cleverly transform the small space into a place of light and beauty. The church, completed in 1641, stands at the intersection known as the **Quattro Fontane,** after the late-16th-century fountains on its four corners, representing Fidelity, Strength and the rivers Arno and Tiber. A clean-up job was completed in 2015, and they look better than they have for years – just watch out for traffic as you admire them. (Via del Quirinale 23; ⊘10am-1pm & 3-6pm Mon-Fri, 10am-1pm Sat, noon-1pm Sun; ▢ Via Nazionale)

Chiesa di Sant'Andrea al Quirinale
CHURCH

4 ⊙ Map p70, C4

It's said that in his old age Bernini liked to come and enjoy the peace of this late-17th-century church, regarded by many as one of his greatest. Faced with severe space limitations, he managed to produce a sense of grandeur by designing an elliptical floor plan with a series of chapels opening onto the central area. (Via del Quirinale 29; ⊙8.30am-noon & 2.30-6pm winter, 9am-noon & 3-6pm summer; 🚇Via Nazionale)

Palazzo del Quirinale
PALACE

5 ⊙ Map p70, B4

Overlooking Piazza del Quirinale, this immense palace is the official residence of Italy's head of state, the Presidente della Repubblica. For almost three centuries it was the pope's summer residence, but in 1870 Pope Pius IX handed the keys over to Italy's new king. Later, in 1948, it was given to the Italian state. (☑06 4 69 91; www.quirinale. it; Piazza del Quirinale; admission €10, ½hr tour €1.50, 2½hr tour €10; ⊙9.30am-4pm Tue, Wed & Fri-Sun, closed Aug; 🚇Barberini)

Scuderie Papali al Quirinale
GALLERY

6 ⊙ Map p70, B4

The Palazzo del Quirinale's former stables, the Scuderie Papali al Quirinale is now a magnificent exhibition space. (☑06 3996 7500; www.scuderiequirinale.it; Via XXIV Maggio 16; tickets around €12)

Galleria Colonna
GALLERY

7 ⊙ Map p70, B4

The only part of Palazzo Colonna open to the public, this opulent 17th-century gallery houses the Colonna family's private art collection. With works by Salvatore Rosa, Guido Reni, Guercino and Annibale Carracci, it's well worth the ticket price. (☑06 678 43 50; www. galleriacolonna.it; Via della Pilotta 17; adult/reduced €12/10; ⊙9am-1.15pm Sat, closed Aug; 🚇Via IV Novembre)

Gagosian Gallery
GALLERY

8 ⊙ Map p70, B2

Since it opened in 2007, the Rome branch of Larry Gagosian's contemporary art empire has hosted the big names of modern art: Cy Twombly, Damien Hirst and Lawrence Weiner, to name a few. The gallery is housed in an artfully converted 1920s bank, and was designed by Roman architect Firouz Galdo and Englishman Caruso St John. (☑06 4208 64 98; www.gagosian. com; Via Francesco Crispi 16; admission free; ⊙10.30am-7pm Tue-Sat; 🚇Barberini)

Galleria d'Arte Moderna
GALLERY

9 ⊙ Map p70, B2

Housed in an 18th-century Carmelite convent, this interesting collection of art and sculpture from the 20th century includes works by de Chirico and Giorgio Morandi. (☑06 06 08; www. galleriaartemodernaroma.it; Via F Crispi 24; adult/reduced €7.50/6.50; ⊙10am-6pm Tue-Sun; 🚇Barberini)

Understand

Rome in Film

Rome has long inspired film-makers, and over the years its historic monuments and seductive piazzas have appeared in everything from neorealist tear-jerkers to art-house classics and sugar-coated rom-coms. Most recently, its cinematic cityscape provided the backdrop to Paolo Sorrentino's 2013 Oscar-winner, *La grande bellezza* (The Great Beauty) and James Bond's escapades in *Spectre* (2015).

Neorealism in the Suburbs

Roberto Rossellini's 1945 masterpiece *Roma Città Aperta* (Rome Open City) was made on location in Rome's battered postwar streets. Filmed in the working-class Prenestina district, it paved the way for films by Vittorio De Sica and Pier Paolo Pasolini, whose *Accattone* (1961) was partly set in the Pigneto neighbourhood.

Scoot Around the Sights

Starring Gregory Peck and Audrey Hepburn, the classic rom-com *Roman Holiday* (1953) presents a more traditional portrait of Rome, featuring sights such as the Colosseum, Roman Forum and Bocca della Verità.

Federico Fellini also made use of Rome's attributes. In *La Dolce Vita* (1960) he had Anita Ekberg dancing in the Trevi Fountain and losing her hat at St Peter's Basilica, while in *Roma* (1972) he takes viewers to some of Rome's most picturesque areas as well as some decidedly unlovely ones, such as the traffic-choked ring road known as the GRA.

Pantheon & Piazzas

The Pantheon has appeared in everything from Peter Greenaway's *Belly of an Architect* (1987) to *Angels and Demons* (2009), which bounces between various locations, including the Chiesa di Santa Maria del Popolo and Piazza Navona; the latter also sets the scene for a midnight ramble in *La grande bellezza*.

Rome's piazzas are a sure thing for directors requiring atmosphere. In *The Talented Mr Ripley* (1999), Piazza di Spagna provides a moneyed setting for the film's glossy characters. Similarly, Trastevere's picturesque piazzas and lanes scream charm in *Barney's Version* (2010) and Woody Allen's *To Rome With Love* (2012).

Convento dei Cappuccini

MUSEUM

10 Map p70, C2

This church and convent complex has turned its extraordinary Capuchin cemetery into cash by adding a flashy museum and bumping up the entrance fee. However, it's still worth visiting what is possibly Rome's strangest sight: crypt chapels where everything from the picture frames to the light fittings is made of human bones. The multimedia museum tells the story of the Capuchin order of monks, including a work attributed to Caravaggio: *St Francis in Meditation*. (☎06 487 11 85; Via Vittorio Veneto 27; adult/reduced €8/6; ⏰9am-7pm; Ⓜ Barberini)

Eating

Colline Emiliane

ITALIAN €€

11 ✗ Map p70, C3

This welcoming, tucked-away restaurant just off Piazza Barberini flies the flag for Emilia-Romagna, the well-fed Italian province that has blessed the world with Parmesan, balsamic vinegar, bolognese sauce and Parma ham. This is a consistently excellent place to eat; there are delicious meats, homemade pasta and rich *ragù* (meat and tomato sauce). Try to save room for dessert too. (☎06 481 75 38; Via degli Avignonesi 22; meals €50; ⏰12.45-2.45pm Tue-Sun & 7.30-10.45pm Tue-Sat, closed Aug; Ⓜ Barberini)

Understand

Bernini & Borromini, Rome's Baroque Rivals

Born within a year of each other, the two giants of Roman baroque hated each other with a vengeance. While Gian Lorenzo Bernini (1598–1680) was an ebullient, urbane player (he seduced the pope's niece to nab the commission for the Fontana dei Quattro Fiumi), Francesco Borromini (1599–1677) was neurotic, reclusive and tortured.

They worked together on St Peter's Basilica and Palazzo Barberini but for most of their careers they competed for commissions and public acclaim. Bernini flourished under Pope Urban VIII (r 1623–44) and Borromini under his successor Innocent X (r 1644–55), but all the while their loathing simmered. Borromini sniffed at Bernini's lack of architectural training while Bernini claimed that Borromini 'had been sent to destroy architecture'.

Of the two, Bernini is generally reckoned to have had the better of the rivalry. His genius was rarely questioned and when he died he was widely regarded as one of Europe's greatest artists. Borromini struggled to win popular and critical support and after a life of depression killed himself in 1677.

Chapel decorated with the bones of Capuchin monks, Convento dei Cappuccini

Baccano
BRASSERIE €€

12 Map p70, A4

Offering all-day dining in elegant, laid-back surroundings (it's nailed the Balthazar look: polished wood, potted palms, high ceilings, cosy booths). However, if you're in the mood: dinner, burgers, club sandwiches, cocktails, *aperitivi* – you name it, they've got it covered. (www.baccanoroma.com; Via delle Muratte 23; meals €45; ⊙8.30am-2am; 🚇Via del Corso)

Il Chianti
TUSCAN €€

13 Map p70, B3

This pretty ivy-clad wine bar is bottle-lined and wood-beamed inside, with watch-the-world-go-by streetside seat-ing, backed by a picturesque cascade of ivy, in summer. Cuisine is Tuscan, so the beef is particularly good, but it also serves up imaginative salads and pizza (for lunch or dinner). (✆06 678 75 50; Via del Lavatore 81-82; meals €45, pizza €8-12; ⊙12.30-3.30pm & 7-11.30pm; 🚇Via del Tritone)

Da Michele
PIZZA €

14 Map p70, A4

A handy address in Spagna district: buy your fresh, crispy *pizza al taglio* (by the slice), and you'll have a delicious fast lunch. It's all kosher, so meat and cheese is not mixed. (✆349 2525347; Via dell'Umiltà 31; pizza slice from €3; ⊙8am-6pm Mon-Fri, to 10pm summer; 🚇Via del Corso)

Understand
Gelato

Eating gelato is as much a part of Roman life as traffic jams and dodgy politicians. And with good reason – the city boasts some fantastic artisanal gelaterie.

No one is quite sure where or when ice cream originated, but it's said that Nero used to snack on snow mixed with fruit pulp and honey, and that the Arabs introduced techniques for making sorbets when they colonised Sicily in the 9th century. Whatever. The fact remains that Italian gelato (slightly denser, softer and less creamy than ice cream) is superb. The best is always made from fresh, seasonal ingredients – so no strawberry in winter – sourced from top-quality producers. And don't be fooled by appearances. Good-quality gelato is not necessarily the prettiest on show: top-notch pistachio ice cream, for example, is a dull ochre-green colour rather than bright, vibrant green. Ditto, banana: bright yellow equals bad, grey is good.

Nanà Vini e Cucina   TRATTORIA €€

15 Map p70, B3

An appealing and simple trattoria, specialising in Neopolitan flavours. Eat in the high-ceilinged interior, under huge brass pipes, overlooking the open kitchen, or outside on the *piazzetta*. Try *la carne tenerera scaloppina Nanà*, cooked simply in white wine, and other southern dishes. (06 6919 0750; Via della Panetteria 37; meals €45; 12.30-3pm & 7-11pm Tue-Sun; Via del Tritone)

Al Moro   ITALIAN €€€

16 Map p70, A4

This one-time Fellini haunt is a step back in time with its picture-gallery dining rooms, Liberty lamps, buttoned-up waiters and old-money regulars. Join faux royals for soothing classics such as *cicoria al brodo* (chicory in broth) or melt-in-your-mouth veal liver with crusty sage and butter. (06 678 34 96; Vicolo delle Bollette 13; meals €55; 1-3.30pm & 8-11.30pm Mon-Sat; Via del Corso)

San Crispino   GELATERIA €

17 Map p70, B3

This is the original place for gourmet gelato, though it has far more rivals in the capital these days. San Crispino, near the Trevi Fountain, serves strictly natural, seasonal flavours. Quality is high, but helpings are on the small side. No cones, as that'd detract from the taste. (06 679 39 24; Via della Panetteria 42; tubs from €2.70; 11am-12.30am Sun-Thu, to 1.30am Fri & Sat; Barberini)

Le Tamerici   SEAFOOD €€€

18 Map p70, B3

Tucked-away Le Tamerici is a cream-hued, elegant escape from the Trevi Fountain hubbub outside. It impresses with its wine list and range of *digestivi*, as well as with its classy food, including light-as-air homemade pasta. The two intimate rooms with beamed ceilings are a suitably discreet place to settle for an epicurean lunch. (☎06 6920 0700; Vicolo Scavolino 79; meals €80; ☺7.30-11pm Mon-Sat, closed Aug; 🚇Via del Tritone)

Drinking

Moma
CAFE

19 🚇 Map p70, D2

Molto trendy: this cafe-restaurant is a find. It's sleekly sexy and popular with workers from nearby offices. There's a small stand-up cafe downstairs, with a nice little deck outside where you can linger longer over coffee and delicious *dolcetti* (sweets). Upstairs is a recommended *cucina creativa* (creative cuisine) restaurant (meals €70). (☎06 4201 1798; Via di San Basilio; ☺8am-midnight Mon-Sat, closed Aug; 🚇Barberini)

Entertainment

Gregory's
LIVE MUSIC

20 ⭐ Map p70, B2

If Gregory's were a tone of voice, it'd be husky: unwind in the downstairs bar, then unwind some more on squashy sofas upstairs to some slinky live jazz and swing, with quality local performers, who also like to hang out here. (☎06 679 63 86; www.gregorysjazz. com; Via Gregoriana 54d; ☺7pm-2am Tue-Sun Sep-Jun; 🚇Barberini, Spagna)

Shopping

Lucia Odescalchi
JEWELLERY

21 🔒 Map p70, A4

If you're looking for a unique piece of statement jewellery, this is the place to head. Housed in the evocative archives of the family *palazzo,* the avant-garde pieces often have an almost medieval beauty, and run from incredible polished steel and chain mail to pieces created out of pearls and fossils. Prices start at around €140. (☎06 6992 5506; Palazzo Odescalchi, Piazza dei Santissimi Apostoli 81; ☺9.30am-2pm Mon-Fri; 🚇Spagna)

Galleria Alberto Sordi
SHOPPING CENTRE

22 🔒 Map p70, A3

This elegant arcade appeared in Alberto Sordi's 1973 classic, *Polvere di Stelle,* and has since been renamed for Rome's favourite actor, who died in 2003. It's a serene place to browse stores such as Zara and Feltrinelli, and there's an airy cafe ideal for a quick coffee break. (Piazza Colonna; ☺10am-10pm; 🚇Via del Corso)

Underground
MARKET

23 🔒 Map p70, B1

Monthly market held underground in a car park near Villa Borghese. There are more than 150 stalls selling everything from antiques and collectables to clothes and toys. (☎06 3600 5345; Ludovisi underground car park, Via Francesco Crispi 96; ☺3-8pm Sat & 10.30am-7.30pm Sun, 2nd weekend of the month Sep-Jun; 🚇Barberini)

Local Life
San Lorenzo & Pigneto

Getting There

🚌 **Bus** Take buses 7 and 492 for San Lorenzo; for Pigneto buses 81, 810, 105 and n12.

🚋 **Tram** Catch tram 3 for San Lorenzo; tram 5, 14 or 19 for Pigneto.

A lively student quarter east of Termini, San Lorenzo is a metropolitan mix of graffiti-clad streets, artists studios, cheap takeaways and hip restaurants. Apart from a major basilica, there are few traditional sights, but come evening the area bursts into life. Southeast, the former working-class Pigneto district is one of the capital's coolest, a bar-heavy pocket frequented by bohemians, hipsters and trend-setting urbanites.

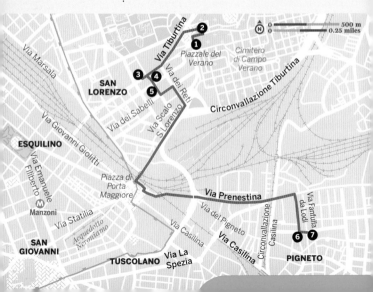

❶ Basilica di San Lorenzo Fuori le Mura

One of Rome's four patriarchal basilicas, the starkly beautiful **Basilica di San Lorenzo Fuori le Mura** (www.basilicasan lorenzo.it; Piazzale San Lorenzo; ⊙8am-noon & 4-6.30pm; 🚊Piazzale del Verano) stands on the site of St Lawrence's burial place. It suffered bomb damage in WWII – the only of the city's major churches to do so – but retains a beautiful Cosmati floor and 13th-century frescoed portico.

❷ Explore the Cimitero di Campo Verano

Next door to the Basilica, the **Cimitero di Campo Verano** (✆06 4923 6349; www.cimiteridiroma.it; Piazzale del Verano; ⊙7.30am-6pm Apr-Sep, to 5pm Oct-Mar; 🚊Piazzale del Verano) is a strangely moving place. Avenues of grandiose tombs criss-cross the cemetery, Rome's largest, which dates to the Napoleonic occupation of Rome (1804–14).

❸ Chocolate at Said

For a change of scene, search out **Said** (✆06 446 92 04; Via Tiburtina 135; meals €50; ⊙10am-12.30am Mon-Thu, to 1.30am Sat & Sun; 🚊Via Tiburtina, 🚊Via dei Reti). A delicious hideaway set in a 1920s factory, it's part shop – selling all sorts of exotic chocs – part bar (try the hot chocolate) and part mod-creative restaurant.

❹ Modern Art at Pastificio Cerere

San Lorenzo's boho credentials express themselves to the full at the **Pastificio Cerere** (✆06 4542 2960; www.pastificiocerere.com; Via degli Ausoni 7; ⊙3-7pm Mon-Fri, 4-8pm Sat; 🚊Via Tiburtina), a former pasta factory turned contemporary art collective. Home to artists studios, a gallery and courtyard space, it hosts regular exhibitions.

❺ Dining at Pommidoro

Unchanged throughout San Lorenzo's metamorphosis from working-class district to bohemian enclave, century-old **Pommidoro** (✆06 445 26 92; Piazza dei Sanniti 44; meals €35; ⊙12.30-3.30pm & 7-11pm Mon-Sat, closed Aug; 🚊Via Tiburtina) is a much-loved local institution specialising in classic Roman pastas and delicious grilled meats.

❻ Hang Out at Necci

Start your exploration of bar-studded Pigneto at iconic **Necci** (✆06 9760 1552; www.necci1924.com; Via Fanfulla da Lodi 68; dinner around €45, lunch mains around €8; ⊙8am-2am; 🛜; 🚊Via Prenestina). The old stomping ground of film director Pier Paolo Pasolini, this laid-back cafe-cum-restaurant caters to an eclectic crowd, who come to drink on the leafy terrace or dine on sophisticated seasonal food.

❼ Cocktails at Co.So

Cocktails are hot in Rome right now and hipster haunt **Co.So** (Via Braccio da Montone 80; cocktails €10; ⊙7pm-3am Mon-Sat; 🚊Via Prenestina) is one of the scene's trend-setters. The drink to try is the Carbonara Sour, a homage to Rome's classic pasta dish made with vodka infused with pork fat.

Explore

Monti & Esquilino

With its village vibe and sloping, cobbled lanes, Monti is one of Rome's coolest quarters. In ancient times it was the city's red-light district but it now plays host to a colourful cast of studios, boutiques, bars and restaurants. Rising to the east, cosmopolitan Esquilino (Esquiline) boasts some amazing churches, one of Rome's best museums, and the transport hub Stazione Termini.

The Sights in a Day

Leave the choking chaos of Termini behind as you enter the hushed halls of the **Museo Nazionale Romano: Palazzo Massimo alle Terme** (p82), one of Rome's best museums. Lose yourself among the sculpture and frescoes before heading over to the **Basilica di Santa Maria Maggiore** (p85) and nearby **Chiesa di Santa Prassede** (p85), famous for its glorious Byzantine mosaics. After so much worthy art, treat yourself to lunch at **Trattoria Monti** (p87).

First stop on the afternoon agenda (but make it after 3pm) is the **Basilica di San Pietro in Vincoli** (p85), boasting a resident Michelangelo. Afterwards, push on to Monti to explore the boutiques and ateliers of **Via del Boschetto** (p90). From the top of the street, make for **Palazzo delle Esposizioni** (p86) to check out an exhibition.

Spend the evening in Monti. Start with dinner at **L'Asino d'Oro** (p87), then take your pick from the area's many bars and cafes – **Ai Tre Scalini** (p89) is always a popular choice.

 Top Sights

Museo Nazionale Romano: Palazzo Massimo alle Terme (p82)

Best of Rome

History
Basilica di San Pietro in Vincoli (p85)

Eating
Open Colonna (p87)

Shopping
Tina Sondergaard (p90)

101 (p91)

Culture
Teatro dell'Opera di Roma (p89)

Charity Café (p90)

Blackmarket (p90)

Getting There

Ⓜ **Metro** For Monti, get off at Cavour on line B. Termini (lines A and B), Castro Pretorio (line B) and Vittorio Emanuele (line A) are useful for Esquilino.

🚌 **Bus** Termini is the city's main bus hub, with connections to all corners of the city. Monti is accessible via buses that stop on Via Nazionale or Via Cavour.

Top Sights
Museo Nazionale Romano: Palazzo Massimo alle Terme

Every day, thousands of tourists, commuters and passers-by hurry past this towering Renaissance *palazzo* (mansion) without giving it a second glance. They don't know what they're missing. This is one of Rome's great museums, an oft-overlooked treasure trove of classical art. The sculpture is truly impressive but what really takes the breath away is the collection of vibrantly coloured frescoes and mosaics.

Map p84, C2

www.coopculture.it

Largo di Villa Peretti 1

adult/reduced €7/3.50

⊙ 9am-7.45pm Tue-Sun

Ⓜ Termini

Mosaic of Hercules and Iolaus

Don't Miss

Sculpture

The ground and 1st floors are devoted to sculpture with some breathtaking pieces. Ground-floor showstoppers include the 5th-century-BC *Niobide morente* (Dying Niobid) and two 2nd-century Greek bronzes – the *Pugile* (Boxer) and the *Principe ellenistico* (Hellenistic Prince). Upstairs, look out for *Il discobolo* (Discus Thrower), a muscular 2nd-century copy of an ancient Greek work. Another admirable body belongs to the graceful *Ermafrodite dormiente* (Sleeping Hermaphrodite).

Frescoes & Mosaics

On the 2nd floor you'll find the museum's thrilling exhibition of ancient mosaics and frescoes. These vibrantly coloured panels were originally used as interior decor and provide a rare picture of how colourful the inside of an upmarket Roman villa must have been. There are intimate *cubicula* (bedroom) frescoes focusing on nature, mythology, domestic and sensual life, and landscape paintings from the winter *triclinium* (dining room).

Villa Livia Frescoes

The museum's crowning glory is this room of frescoes from Villa Livia, one of the homes of Augustus' wife Livia Drusilla. The paintings, which originally decorated a summer *triclinium,* depict a paradisiacal garden full of roses, violets, pomegranates, irises and camomile under a deep-blue sky.

Basement

The basement contains a coin collection that's far more absorbing than you might expect, tracing the Roman Empire's use of coins for propaganda purposes. There's also the disturbing remains of a mummified eight-year-old girl, the only known example of mummification from the Roman Empire.

HERITAGE IMAGES/GETTY IMAGES ©

☑ Top Tips

▶ Start your visit on the 2nd floor, so you can see the amazing mosaics and frescoes when you're fresh.

▶ Remember that your ticket is valid for three days and provides admission to the other three sites of the Museo Nazionale Romano.

▶ The museum often stages excellent temporary exhibitions. If there's one on, you'll have to pay a €3 supplement on top of the regular ticket price.

✗ Take a Break

Revive sagging energy levels with a sugar fix from the historic Pasticceria Regoli (p88). Alternatively, drop into Panella L'Arte del Pane (p88) for a coffee and gourmet snack.

For reviews see

◉	Top Sights	p82
◎	Sights	p85
✖	Eating	p87
🍷	Drinking	p89
★	Entertainment	p89
🔒	Shopping	p90

Sights

Basilica di Santa Maria Maggiore

BASILICA

1 Map p84, C3

One of Rome's four patriarchal basilicas, this monumental 5th-century church stands on the Esquiline Hill, on the spot where snow is said to have miraculously fallen in the summer of AD 358. Much altered over the centuries, it has a 14th-century Romanesque belfry, an 18th-century baroque facade, a largely baroque interior, and a series of glorious 5th-century mosaics. (Piazza Santa Maria Maggiore; basilica/museum/ loggia/archaeological site free/€3/5/5; ⊘7am-7pm, museum & loggia 9am-5.30pm; ▣Piazza Santa Maria Maggiore)

Chiesa di Santa Prassede

CHURCH

2 Map p84, C4

Famous for its brilliant mosaics, this church is dedicated to St Praxedes, an early Christian heroine who hid Christians fleeing persecution and buried those she couldn't save in a well. The position of the well is now marked by a marble disc on the floor of the nave. (Via Santa Prassede 9a; ⊘7.30am-noon & 4-6.30pm; ▣Piazza Santa Maria Maggiore)

Basilica di San Pietro in Vincoli

BASILICA

3 Map p84, B5

Pilgrims and art lovers flock to this 5th-century basilica for two reasons:

to marvel at Michelangelo's colossal *Moses* (1505) sculpture and to see the chains that supposedly bound St Peter when he was imprisoned in the Carcere Mamertino (near the Roman Forum). Access to the church is via a flight of steps through a low arch that leads up from Via Cavour. (Piazza di San Pietro in Vincoli 4a; ⊘8am-12.20pm & 3-7pm summer, to 6pm winter; ▣Cavour)

Domus Aurea

ARCHAEOLOGICAL SITE

4 Map p84, A5

Nero had his Domus Aurea constructed after the fire of AD 64 (which it's rumoured he had started to clear the area). Named after the gold that lined its facade and interiors, it was a huge complex covering up to a third of the city. The excavated part of the site has been repeatedly closed due to flooding, but opened for weekend guided tours from late 2014; check the website for its current opening status. (Golden House; ☎06 3996 7700; www.coop culture.it; Viale della Domus Aurea; admisson/ with online booking fee €10/12; ⊘guided tours Sat & Sun; ▣Colosseo)

Museo Nazionale Romano: Terme di Diocleziano

MUSEUM

5 Map p84, D1

The Terme di Diocleziano was ancient Rome's largest bath complex, covering about 13 hectares and with a capacity for 3000 people. Today its ruins constitute part of the impressive Museo Nazionale Romano. This branch of the National Roman Museum supplies a fascinating insight into Roman life through memorial inscriptions and other artefacts. Outside, the vast, elegant cloister was constructed from drawings by Michelangelo. (☏06 3996 7700; www.coopculture.it; Viale Enrico de Nicola 78; adult/reduced €7/3.50; ⊙9am-7.30pm Tue-Sun; Ⓜ Termini)

Museo Nazionale d'Arte Orientale

MUSEUM

6 ◉ Map p84, D4

This little-visited but impressive collection is housed in the grandiose 19th-century Palazzo Brancaccio. It includes 5th-century-BC Iranian glassware, items from the ancient settlement of Swat in Pakistan, 12th-century homewares from Afghanistan, engraved ritual vessels from China dating from 800 BC to 900 BC, and a new Korean gallery with bronzes, seals and contemporary art. (☏06 4697 4823; www.museorientale.beniculturali.it; Via Merulana 248; adult/reduced €6/3; ⊙9am-2pm Tue, Wed & Fri, 9am-7.30pm Thu, Sat & Sun; Ⓜ Vittorio Emanuele)

Palazzo delle Esposizioni

CULTURAL CENTRE

7 ◉ Map p84, A2

This huge neoclassical palace was built in 1882 as an exhibition centre, though it has since served as headquarters for the Italian Communist Party, a mess hall for Allied servicemen, a polling station and even a public loo. Nowadays it's a splendid cultural hub, with cathedral-scale exhibition spaces hosting blockbuster art exhibitions and sleekly designed art labs, as well as a bookshop and cafe. (☏06 3996 7500;

Understand

Legend of the Magic Door

Set in the heart of Esquilino a short hop south from Stazione Termini, por-ticoed **Piazza Vittorio Emanuele II** is Rome's largest square (Piazza San Pietro is in the Vatican, so it doesn't count). Amid the ruins in the fenced-off central section, you'll see a mysterious doorway covered in cabbalistic symbols. This is the **Porta Magica**, a door that once led to Villa Palombara, which stood here until the late 19th century.

According to legend, the villa's owner, the Marquis Palombara, had financed a young necromancer named Giuseppe Francesco Borri, who was set on discovering the philosopher's stone (which turns matter into gold). But Borri vanished one day, leaving behind a pile of papers inscribed with secret formulae that the marquis hoped would unlock the magic formula. When even the best alchemists were left scratching their heads, Palombara engraved the symbols into the doorway, hoping that an expert would one day see them and finally crack the code.

www.palazzoesposizioni.it; Via Nazionale 194; ⊙10am-8pm Tue-Thu & Sun, to 10.30pm Fri & Sat; 🚇Via Nazionale)

Piazza della Repubblica   PIAZZA

8 📍 Map p84, C1

Flanked by grand 19th-century neo-classical colonnades, this landmark piazza was laid out as part of Rome's postunification makeover. It follows the lines of the semicircular *exedra* (benched portico) of Diocletian's baths complex and was originally known as Piazza Esedra. (🚇Repubblica)

Eating

Open Colonna   ITALIAN €€€

9 🍴 Map p84, A2

Spectacularly set at the back of Palazzo delle Esposizioni, superchef Antonello Colonna's superb restaurant is tucked onto a mezzanine floor under an extraordinary glass roof. The cuisine is new Roman: innovative takes on traditional dishes, cooked with wit and flair. The best thing? There's a more basic but still delectable fixed two-course lunch for €16, and Saturday and Sunday brunch is €30, served in the dramatic, glass-ceilinged hall, with a terrace for sunny days. (📞06 4782 2641; www.antonellocolonna.it; Via Milano 9a; meals €20-80; ⊙12.30-3.30pm Tue-Sun, 8-11.30pm Tue-Sat; ❄; 🚇Via Nazionale)

L'Asino d'Oro   ITALIAN €€

10 🍴 Map p84, A3

This fabulous restaurant was transplanted from Orvieto and its Umbrian origins resonate in Lucio Sforza's exceptional cooking. It's unfussy yet innovative, with dishes featuring lots of flavourful contrasts, such as lamb meatballs with pear and blue cheese. Save room for the amazing desserts. For such excellent food, this intimate, informal yet classy place is one of Rome's best deals. Hours are changeable so call ahead. (📞06 4891 3832; Via del Boschetto 73; meals €45; ⊙12.30-2.30pm Sat, 7.30-11pm Tue-Sat; 🚇Cavour)

Trattoria Monti   RISTORANTE €€

11 🍴 Map p84, D4

The Camerucci family runs this elegant brick-arched place, proffering top-notch traditional cooking from the Marches region. There are wonderful *fritti* (fried things), delicate pastas and ingredients such as *pecorino di fossa* (sheep's milk cheese aged in caves), goose, swordfish and truffles. Try the egg-yolk *tortelli* pasta. Desserts are delectable, including apple pie with *zabaglione* (egg and marsala custard). Word has spread, so book ahead. (📞06 446 65 73; Via di San Vito 13a; meals €45; ⊙12.45-2.45pm Tue-Sun, 7.45-11pm Tue-Sat, closed Aug; 🚇Vittorio Emanuele)

Local Life

Pasticceria Regoli

Italian tradition dictates that you take a tray of pastries and small cakes to mamma's for Sunday lunch. And much-loved **Pasticceria Regoli** (Map p84, D4; Via dello Statuto 60; ☉6.30am-8.20pm Wed-Sun; ⓂVittorio Emanuele) is where the locals come to buy theirs. But you don't need an occasion to stop by – just being in Rome is reason enough.

Temakinho   SUSHI €€

12   Map p84, A4

In a city where food is still mostly resolutely (though deliciously) Italian, this Brazilian-Japanese hybrid serves up sushi and ceviche, and makes for a refreshing, sensational change. As well as delicious, strong *caipirinhas*, which combine Brazilian *cachaça*, sugar, lime and fresh fruit, there are '*sakehinhas*' made with sake. It's very popular; book ahead. (www.temakinho.com; Via dei Serpenti 16; meals €40; ☉12.30-3.30pm & 7pm-midnight; ⓂCavour)

Panella l'Arte del Pane   BAKERY, CAFE €

13   Map p84, D4

With a magnificent array of *pizza al taglio* (by the slice), *arancini* (deep-fried rice balls stuffed with meat, cheese and vegetables), focaccia, fried croquettes and pastries, this smart bakery-cum-cafe is good any time of the day. The outside tables are ideal for a leisurely breakfast or chilled evening drink, or you can perch on a high stool and lunch on something from the sumptuous counter display. (☏06 487 24 35; Via Merulana 54; snacks about €3.50; ☉8am-11pm Mon-Thu, to midnight Fri & Sat, 8.30am-4pm Sun; ⓂVittorio Emanuele)

Ciuri Ciuri   PASTRIES €

14   Map p84, A4

Oh *yes*...what's not to love about a Sicilian ice-cream and pastry shop? Pop by for delectable homemade sweets such as freshly filled *cannoli* (ricotta-filled tubes), *cassata* (a cake, cream, marzipan, chocolate and candied fruit concoction) and *pasticini di mandorla* (almond pastries), all available in bite-sized versions. It's not all sweet: there are also excellent freshly made *arancini* and other snacks. Eat in or out. (☏06 4544 4548; Via Leonina 18; snacks around €3; ☉8.30am-midnight Sun-Thu, to 2am Fri & Sat; ⓂCavour)

Da Valentino   TRATTORIA €€

15   Map p84, A3

The vintage 1930s sign outside says 'Birra Peroni', and inside the lovely old-fashioned feel indicates that not much has changed here for years, with black-and-white photographs on the walls, white tablecloths and tiled floors. Come here when you're in the mood for grilled *scamorza* (a type of Italian cheese, similar to mozzarella), as this is the main focus of the menu, with myriad variations: served with tomato and rocket, tomato and gorgonzola, cheese and artichokes, grilled meats, hamburgers and so on. (06 488 06 43; Via del Boschetto; meals €25-30; 🕐1-2.45pm & 7.30-11.30pm Mon-Sat; 🅼Cavour)

Drinking

Ai Tre Scalini
WINE BAR

16 Map p84, A4

The 'Three Steps' is always packed, with crowds spilling out into the street. Apart from a tasty choice of wines, it sells the damn fine Menabrea beer, brewed in northern Italy. You can also tuck into an array of cheeses, salami and dishes such as *polpette al sugo* (meatballs with sauce; €7.50). (Via Panisperna 251; 🕐12.30pm-1am; 🅼Cavour)

Fafiuché
WINE BAR

17 🍺 Map p84, A4

Fafiuché means 'light-hearted fun' in the Piedmontese dialect, and this place lives up to its name. The narrow, bottle-lined orange space exudes charm: come here to enjoy wine and artisanal beers, eat delicious dishes originating from Puglia to Piedmont, or buy delectable foodstuffs. *Aperitivo* (bar buffet) is from 6.30pm to 9pm. (📞06 699 09 68; www.fafiuche.it; Via della Madonna dei Monti 28; 🕐5.30pm-1am Mon-Sat; 🅼Cavour)

La Bottega del Caffè
CAFE

18 🍺 Map p84, A4

Ideal for frittering away any balmy section of the day, this appealing cafe-

bar, named after a comedy by Carlo Goldoni, has greenery-screened tables out on the pretty Piazza Madonna dei Monti. It serves snacks, from simple pizzas to cheeses and salamis. (Piazza Madonna dei Monti 5; 🕐8am-2am; 🅼Cavour)

La Barrique
WINE BAR

19 Map p84, A3

This appealing *enoteca,* with wooden furniture and whitewashed walls, is a classy yet informal place to hang out and sample excellent French, Italian and German wines; a choice of perfectly cooked, delicious main courses provide a great accompaniment, or you can stick to artisanal cheeses and cold cuts. (Via del Boschetto 41b; 🕐12.30-3.30pm & 5.30pm-1am Mon-Sat; 🅼Cavour)

Entertainment

Teatro dell'Opera di Roma
OPERA

20 Map p84, C2

Rome's premier opera house boasts a plush and gilt interior, a Fascist 1920s exterior and an impressive history: it premiered Puccini's *Tosca,* and Maria Callas once sang here. Opera and ballet performances are staged between September and June. (📞06 481 70 03; www.operaroma.it; Piazza Beniamino Gigli; ballet €12-80, opera €17-150; 🕐9am-5pm Tue-Sat, to 1.30pm Sun; 🅼Repubblica)

Blackmarket
LIVE MUSIC

21 Map p84, B3

A bit outside the main Monti hub, this charming, living-room-style bar filled with eclectic vintage furniture is great for sitting back on mismatched armchairs for a leisurely, convivial drink. It hosts regular acoustic music and folk gigs, which feel a bit like having a band in your living room. (www.black-market.it; Via Panisperna 101; ⏰5.30pm-2am; Ⓜ Cavour)

Local Life

Shopping on Via del Boschetto

While Monti has no shortage of cool streets, **Via del Boschetto** (Map p84, A4) is the stand-out strip. Its eclectic boutiques and bric-a-brac boltholes are perfect for picking up vintage clothes, costume jewellery and one-off fashions, all at affordable prices.

At No 148, **Fabio Piccioni** (☎06 474 16 97; Via del Boschetto 148; ⏰10.30am-1pm Tue-Sat, 2-8pm Mon-Sat; Ⓜ Cavour) is known for his deco-inspired jewellery crafted from old trinkets. Further up, at No 1d, Danish designer **Tina Sondergaard** (☎334 3850799; Via del Boschetto 1d; ⏰3-7.30pm Mon, 10.30am-7.30pm Tue-Sat, closed Aug; Ⓜ Cavour) has built a reputation creating limited-edition retro ladies wear. At No 6 **Spot** (☎338 9275739; Via del Boschetto; ⏰10.30am-7.30pm Mon-Sat; Ⓜ Cavour) specialises in cool design homeware.

Charity Café
LIVE MUSIC

22 Map p84, A3

Think narrow space, spindly tables, dim lighting and a laid-back vibe: this is a place to snuggle down and listen to some slinky live jazz. Civilised, relaxed, untouristy and very Monti. Gigs usually take place from 10pm, with live music and *aperitivo* on Sundays. There's open mic from 7pm on Monday and Tuesday. (☎328 8452915; www.charitycafe.it; Via Panisperna 68; ⏰7pm-2am; Ⓜ Cavour)

Shopping

Mercato Monti Urban Market
MARKET

23 Map p84, A4

Vintage clothes, accessories, one-off pieces by local designers, this market in the hip hood of Monti is well worth a rummage. (www.mercatomonti.com; Via Leonina 46; ⏰10am-8pm Sat & Sun; Ⓜ Cavour)

La Bottega del Cioccolato
FOOD

24 Map p84, A4

Run by the younger generation of Moriondo & Gariglio (p52), this is a magical world of scarlet walls and old-fashioned glass cabinets set into black wood, with irresistible smells wafting in from the kitchen and rows of lovingly homemade chocolates on display. (☎06 482 14 73; Via Leonina 82; ⏰9.30am-7.30pm Oct-Aug; Ⓜ Cavour)

IMAGE COURTESY OF MERCATO MONTI

Mercato Monti Urban Market

101
CLOTHING

25 🔒 Map p84, B4

The collection at this boutique might include gossamer-light jumpers, broad-brimmed hats, chain-mail earrings and silk dresses: it's always worth a look to discover a special something. (Via Urbana; ⏰10am-1.30pm & 2-8pm; Ⓜ️Cavour)

Abito
CLOTHING

26 🔒 Map p84, A3

Wilma Silvestre designs elegant clothes with a difference. Choose from the draped, chic, laid-back styles on the rack, and you can have one made up just for you in a day or just a few hours – customise the fabric and the colour. There's usually one guest designer's clothes also being sold at the shop. (📞06 488 10 17; abito61.blogspot. co.uk; Via Panisperna 61; ⏰10.30am-8pm Mon-Sat, noon-8pm Sun; Ⓜ️Cavour)

Giacomo Santini
SHOES

27 🔒 Map p84, C3

Close to the Basilica di Santa Maria Maggiore, this Fausto Santini outlet store is named after the accessory designer's father, Giacomo. It sells discounted Fausto Santini boots, shoes and bags, and has bargain signature architectural designs in butter-soft leather at a fraction of the retail price. Sizes are limited, however. (📞06 488 09 34; Via Cavour 106; ⏰3.30-7.30pm Mon, 10am-1pm & 3.30-7.30pm Tue-Sat; Ⓜ️Cavour)

Top Sights
Appian Way

Getting There

The Appian Way runs southeast from Porta San Sebastiano, south of the Celio.

🚌 **Bus** Take bus 660 from Colli Albani metro (line A) or 118 from Piramide (line B).

Completed in 190 BC, ancient Rome's *regina viarum* (queen of roads) connected the capital with Brindisi on Italy's southern Adriatic coast. Nowadays, Via Appia Antica is one of Rome's most exclusive addresses, a beautiful cobbled thoroughfare flanked by grassy fields, ancient ruins and towering pine trees. But it has a dark history – it was here that Spartacus and 6000 of his slave rebels were crucified, and the early Christians buried their dead in the underground catacombs.

Bas-relief on the Appian Way

Don't Miss

Mausoleo di Cecilia Metella

Dating back to the 1st century BC, the drum-like **Mausoleo di Cecilia Metella** (☎06 3996 7700; www.coopculture.it; Via Appia Antica 161; adult/reduced incl Terme di Caracalla & Villa dei Quintili €7/4; ☉9am-1hr before sunset Tue-Sun; 🚇Via Appia Antica) was built as a burial chamber for the daughter of the consul Quintus Metellus Creticus. In the 14th century it was fortified by the Caetani family.

Villa di Massenzio

The highlight of **Villa di Massenzio** (☎06 780 13 24; www.villadimassenzio.it; Via Appia Antica 153; ☉9am-1pm Tue-Sat; 🚇Via Appia Antica), Maxentius' 4th-century imperial palace, is the **Circo di Massenzio**, Rome's best-preserved chariot racetrack. The palace's unexcavated ruins sit above the racetrack's northern end. Nearby, Maxentius built the imposing **Mausoleo di Romolo** for his son.

Basilica & Catacombe di San Sebastiano

The **Catacombe di San Sebastiano** (☎06 785 03 50; www.catacombe.org; Via Appia Antica 136; adult/reduced €8/5; ☉10am-5pm Mon-Sat, closed Dec; 🚇Via Appia Antica) boast three perfectly preserved mausoleums with original 2nd-century frescoes, mosaics and stucco. Above ground, the much-tweaked 4th-century **basilica** preserves one of the arrows allegedly used to kill St Sebastian, and the column to which he was tied.

☎06 513 53 16

www.parcoappiaantica.it

🚇Via Appia Antica

☑ Top Tips

▶ The best section of the road – traffic-free on Sundays – is near the Basilica di San Sebastiano.

▶ Get info on tours and bike hire from the **Appia Antica Regional Park Information Point** (☎06 513 53 16; www.parcoappiaantica.it; Via Appia Antica 58-60; ☉9.30am-1pm & 2-5.30pm Mon-Sat, to 5pm winter, 9.30am-6.30pm Sun, to 5pm winter; 🚇Via Appia Antica).

▶ If you're short on time, hit Villa di Massenzio and the nearby Catacombe di San Sebastiano.

✗ Take a Break

Head to **Qui Non se More Mai** (☎06 780 39 22; Via Appia Antica 198; meals around €40; ☉12.30-3pm & 6.30-11.30pm Tue-Sat; 🚇Via Appia Antica) for grilled meats and authentic Roman pastas, situated just south of the Mausoleo di Cecilia Metella on Via Appia Antica.

Understand

The Catacombs

Built as communal burial grounds, the catacombs were the early Christians' solution to the problem of what to do with their dead. Belief in the Resurrection meant that they couldn't cremate their corpses, as was the custom at the time, and ancient Roman law forbade burial within the city walls. Furthermore, as a persecuted minority they didn't have their own cemeteries. So, in the 2nd century they began to dig beneath Via Appia Antica, where a number of converted Christians already had family tombs.

Over time, as Christianity became more popular, competition for burial space became fierce and a cut-throat trade in tomb real estate developed. However, by the late 4th century, Christianity had been legalised and the Christians began to bury their dead near the basilicas within the city walls. By the Middle Ages the catacombs had been all but abandoned.

Catacombe di San Callisto

The largest and busiest of Rome's catacombs, the 2nd-century **Catacombe di San Callisto** (☎06 513 01 51; www.catacombe.roma.it; Via Appia Antica 110 & 126; adult/reduced €8/5; ☉9am-noon & 2-5pm, closed Wed & Feb; ◻Via Appia Antica) served as the first official cemetery of the Roman Church. In the 20km of tunnels explored to date, archaeologists have found the tombs of 500,000 people and seven martyred popes.

Catacombe di Santa Domitilla

Among Rome's oldest, the **Catacombe di Santa Domitilla** (☎06 511 03 42; www.domitilla.info; Via delle Sette Chiese 283; adult/reduced €8/5; ☉9am-noon & 2-5pm Wed-Mon, closed Jan; ◻Via Appia Antica) extend for about 18km. They contain Christian wall paintings and the haunting underground **Chiesa di SS Nereus e Achilleus**, a 4th-century church dedicated to two Roman soldiers martyred by Diocletian.

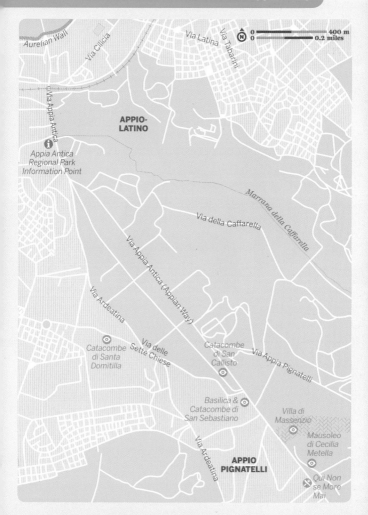

Aurelian Wall

Via Cilicia

Via Latina

Via Tabarini

N

0   400 m
0   0.2 miles

Via Appia Antica

**APPIO-
LATINO**

Appia Antica
Regional Park
Information Point

Marrana della Caffarella

Via della Caffarella

Via Appia Antica (Appian Way)

Via Ardeatina

Via delle
Sette Chiese

Catacombe
di Santa
Domitilla

Catacombe
di San
Callisto

Via Appia Pignatelli

Basilica &
Catacombe di
San Sebastiano

Villa di
Massenzio

Mausoleo
di Cecilia
Metella

Via Ardeatina

**APPIO
PIGNATELLI**

Qui Non
se More
Mai

Explore

San Giovanni & Celio

Southeast of the centre, the mighty Basilica di San Giovanni in Laterano is the principal drawcard of the handsome, largely residential San Giovanni district. Nearby, the Celio (Caelian), one of Rome's original seven hills, rises to the south of the Colosseum. A tranquil area of medieval churches and graceful greenery, it's ideal for escaping the crowds but offers little after-hours action.

The Sights in a Day

☀ Hop on the metro and head to San Giovanni. Exit the station, pass through Porta San Giovanni, and there, on your left, you'll see the great white **Basilica di San Giovanni in Laterano** (p98). Once you've explored its interior and lovely cloister, stop off at **Via Sannio market** (p105) to look for a bargain, before doubling back to the **Basilica di San Clemente** (p101) and its creepy underground corridors. Lunch at laid-back **Cafè Cafè** (p103).

☀ After you've eaten, head to **Villa Celimontana** (p102; pictured left) to wait for the nearby **Chiesa di Santo Stefano Rotondo** (p102) to open. Study the church's grisly frescoes to see what fate lay in store for the early Christian martyrs, some of whom supposedly lived in the **Case Romane** (p103) under the Chiesa di SS Giovanni e Paolo.

☾ Finish the day off with a wood-fired pizza at **Li Rioni** (p103) and jazz-fuelled drinks at **Il Pentagrappolo** (p104). Alternatively, feast on Colosseum views and classy, contemporary cuisine at rooftop **Aroma** (p103).

◉ Top Sights

Basilica di San Giovanni in Laterano (p98)

♥ Best of Rome

History

Basilica di San Clemente (p101)

Case Romane (p103)

Basilica di San Giovanni in Laterano (p98)

Eating

Aroma (p103)

Gay & Lesbian

Coming Out (p104)

Getting There

Ⓜ **Metro** San Giovanni is accessible by metro line A. For the Celio, you can walk up from Colosseo or Circo Massimo stations (both line B).

🚍 **Bus** Buses that stop near the Basilica di San Giovanni in Laterano include bus 85, which heads up Via Appia Nuova to Termini; bus 87, which runs between Prati and Colli Albani; and bus 714, which links Termini with EUR.

Top Sights
Basilica di San Giovanni in Laterano

For a thousand years this monumental cathedral was the most important church in Christendom. Consecrated in AD 324, it was the first Christian basilica to be built in Rome and, until the 14th century, was the pope's main place of worship. It's still Rome's official cathedral and the pope's seat as the bishop of Rome. The oldest of Rome's four papal basilicas, it has twice been destroyed by fire and the church you see today is a culmination of several comprehensive makeovers.

👁 Map p100, E3

Piazza di San Giovanni in Laterano 4

basilica/cloister free/€5

🕓 7am–6.30pm, cloister 9am–6pm

Ⓜ San Giovanni

Decorations in the nave

Don't Miss

The Facade

Surmounted by 15 7m-high statues – Christ with St John the Baptist, John the Evangelist and the 12 Apostles – Alessandro Galilei's immense late-baroque facade was added in 1735. In the portico, the central **bronze doors** were moved here from the Curia in the Roman Forum, while on the far right, the **Holy Door** is only ever opened in Jubilee years.

The Nave

The echoing, marble-clad interior owes much of its present look to Francesco Borromini who redecorated it for the 1650 Jubilee. It's a breath-taking sight with a golden gilt ceiling and a wide central nave lined with 18th-century sculptures of the apostles, each 4.6m high and each set in a heroic pose in its own dramatic niche.

The Baldachin & Apse

At the head of the nave, an elaborate Gothic baldachin towers over the papal altar. Dating to the 14th century, it's said to contain the relics of St Peter's and St Paul's heads. In front, a double staircase leads down to the **confessio** and the Renaissance tomb of Pope Martin V.

The Cloister

To the left of the altar, the basilica's 13th-century cloister is a lovely, peaceful place with graceful twisted columns set around a central garden. Lining the ambulatories are marble fragments from the original church, including the remains of a 5th-century papal throne and inscriptions of two papal bulls.

☑ Top Tips

▶ Audioguides are available for a voluntary donation from a desk in the central nave.

▶ Look down as well as up – the basilica has a beautiful 15th-century inlaid mosaic floor.

▶ It's worth paying the fee to enter the peaceful cloister.

▶ Check out the Giotto fresco on the first column in the right-hand nave.

▶ For a virtual tour of the basilica, plus an ecclesiastical soundtrack, check out www.vatican.va/various/basiliche/san_giovanni/vr_tour/index-it.html.

✕ Take a Break

There are few recommended eateries right by the basilica, so you're better off finishing your tour and heading downhill towards the Colosseum. Here you can lunch on classic trattoria food at Il Bocconcino (p103) or tasty cafe fare at Cafè Cafè (p103).

E Manzoni
Via di Quintino
Via di Quintino
Viale Manzoni
Via Nino Bixio
Viale Manzoni

San Giovanni
Piazzale
Appio

Via Veio
Via Magna Grecia

Via Emanuele Filiberto
Via Statilia

Santuario della
Scala Santa & Sancta
Sanctorum

Piazza
di Porta
San Giovanni

18 San Giovanni

Via Amiterno

Via Tasso

Palazzo di
Laterano

Basilica di
San Giovanni
in Laterano

Via Sanio

Via Tasso

Via Bolardo

Obelisk

Piazza di San
Giovanni in Laterano

Battistero

400 m
0.2 miles

Via Manzoni

Via Galilei

Via Merulana

SAN
GIOVANNI

Via Licia

For reviews see
◉ Top Sights   p98
◉ Sights   p101
⊗ Eating   p103
▶ Drinking   p104
🛍 Shopping   p105

Via Alfieri

Via Guicciardini

Via Ruggero Bonghi
Piazza
Iside

Via Labicana

Via di San
Giovanni in Laterano

Via dei Santissimi Quattro Coronati

Via di Santo Stefano Rotondo

Via Ferratella in Laterano

Via dell'Amba Aradam

Via Ipponio

Via di Sant'Erasmo

Via Gallia

Piazzale
Metronia

Via Mecenate

Via Crescimbeni

Via Muratori
Piazza di
San Clemente

Basilica di
San Clemente

Basilica di
SS Quattro
Coronati

Via Annia

Via Celimontana

Chiesa di
Santo Stefano
Rotondo

Piazza
Porta
Metronia

Via dei
Normanni

Via N Salvi

Parco del Colle Oppio

Viale della Domus Aurea

Via dei SS Quattro Coronati

Via di Santo Stefano Rotondo

Via della Navicella

Via della Croce

Via Claudia

CELIO

Villa
Celimontana

Via di Valle delle Camene

Viale delle Terme
di Caracalla

Colosseo

Piazza del
Colosseo

Via Celio Vibenna

Viale del Parco del Celio

CAMPITELLI

Case Romane

Clivo di Scauro

Piazza di
SS Giovanni
e Paolo

Parco
San
Sebastiano

Parco
delle Terme
di Caracalla

Sights

Palazzo Laterano
HISTORIC BUILDING

1 ◎ Map p100, D3

Adjacent to the Basilica di San Giovanni in Laterano, Palazzo Laterano was the official papal residence until the pope moved to the Vatican in 1377. It's still technically Vatican property and today houses offices of the Vicariate of Rome. Much altered over the centuries, it owes its current form to a 16th-century facelift by Domenico Fontana. Overlooking the *palazzo* (mansion) is Rome's oldest and tallest **obelisk**. (Piazza di San Giovanni in Laterano; M San Giovanni)

Santuario della Scala Santa & Sancta Sanctorum
CHAPEL

2 ◎ Map p100, E2

The Scala Sancta, said to be the staircase that Jesus walked up in Pontius Pilate's Jerusalem palace, was brought to Rome by St Helena in the 4th century. Pilgrims consider it sacred and climb it on their knees, saying a prayer on each of the 28 steps. At the top, the richly frescoed Sancta Sanctorum (Holy of Holies) was formerly the pope's private chapel. (www.scala-santa.it; Piazza di San Giovanni in Laterano 14; admission Scala free, Sancta with/without audioguide €5/3.50; ☼ Scala 6am-1pm & 3-7pm summer, to 6.30pm winter, Sancta Sanctorum 9.30am-12.40pm & 3-5.10pm Mon-Sat; M San Giovanni)

Battistero
CHAPEL

3 ◎ Map p100, D3

Built by Constantine in the 4th century, this octagonal baptistry served as the prototype for later Christian churches and bell towers. Most interesting, apart from the architecture, are the decorative mosaics, some of which date to the 5th century. (Piazza di San Giovanni in Laterano; ☼ 9am-12.30pm & 4-6.30pm; M San Giovanni)

Basilica di San Clemente
BASILICA

4 ◎ Map p100, B2

Nowhere better illustrates the various stages of Rome's turbulent past than this fascinating multilayered church. The ground-level 12th-century basilica sits atop a 4th-century church, which, in turn, stands over a 2nd-century pagan temple and a 1st-century Roman house. Beneath everything are foundations dating from the Roman Republic. (www.basilicasanclemente.com; Via di San Giovanni in Laterano; excavations adult/reduced €10/5; ☼ 9am-12.30pm & 3-6pm Mon-Sat, 12.15-6pm Sun; ⬚ Via Labicana)

Basilica di SS Quattro Coronati
BASILICA

5 ◎ Map p100, C2

This brooding fortified church harbours some lovely 13th-century frescoes and a delightful hidden cloister. The frescoes, in the **Oratorio di San Silvestro**, depict the story of the Donation of Constantine, a notorious forged document with which the emperor Constantine ceded control of Rome to the papacy. To access the Oratorio, ring the bell in the entrance courtyard. You might also have to ring for the cloister, which is situated off the northern aisle. (Via dei Santissimi Quattro Coronati 20; ⏱10-11.45am & 4-5.45pm Mon-Sat, 4-5.45pm Sun; 🚇Via di San Giovanni in Laterano)

Chiesa di Santo Stefano Rotondo CHURCH

6 📍 Map p100, B3

Set in its own secluded grounds, this haunting church boasts a porticoed facade and a round, columned interior. But what really gets the heart racing is the graphic wall decor – a cycle of 16th-century frescoes depicting the tortures suffered by many early Christian martyrs. Describing them in 1846, Charles Dickens wrote: 'Such a panorama of horror and butchery no man could imagine in his sleep, though he were to eat a whole pig, raw, for supper.' (www.santo-stefano-rotondo.it; Via di Santo Stefano Rotondo 7; ⏱10am-1pm & 2-5pm winter, 10am-1pm & 3-6pm summer; 🚇Via della Navicella)

Villa Celimontana PARK

7 📍 Map p100, A3

With its grassy banks and colourful flower beds, this leafy park is a wonderful place to escape the crowds and enjoy a summer picnic. At its centre is a 16th-century villa housing the Italian Geographical Society. (⏱7am-sunset; 🚇Via della Navicella)

Understand

Donation of Constantine

The frescoes in the Basilica di SS Quattro Coronati tell the story of the Donation of Constantine. The Donation, the most famous forgery in medieval history, was a document with which the Roman Emperor Constantine purportedly granted Pope Sylvester I (r AD 314–35) and his successors control of Rome and the Western Roman Empire, as well as primacy over the holy sees of Antioch, Alexandria, Constantinople, Jerusalem and all the world's churches. The alleged motive for Constantine's generosity was his gratitude to Sylvester for having cured him of leprosy.

No one is exactly sure when the document was written but the consensus is that it dates to the mid- or late-8th century. Certainly this fits with the widespread theory that the author was a Roman cleric, possibly working with the knowledge of Pope Stephen II (r 752–57).

For centuries the Donation was accepted as genuine and used by popes to justify their territorial claims. But in 1440 the philosopher Lorenzo Valla proved that it was a forgery. By analysing the language used in the document he was able to show that it was inconsistent with the Latin used in the 4th century.

Case Romane

CHRISTIAN SITE

8 Map p100, A3

According to tradition, the apostles John and Paul lived in these subterranean houses beneath the Basilica di SS Giovanni e Paolo before they were beheaded by the emperor Julian. There's actually no direct evidence of this, although research has revealed that the houses were used for Christian worship. There are more than 20 rooms, many of them richly decorated. Entry is to the side of the basilica on the Clivo di Scauro. (06 7045 4544; www.caseromane.it; adult/reduced €6/4; 10am-1pm & 3-6pm Thu-Mon; Via Claudia)

Eating

Cafè Cafè

BISTRO €

9 Map p100, B2

Cosy, relaxed and welcoming, this cafe-bistro is a far cry from the usual impersonal eateries in the Colosseum area. With its rustic wooden tables, butternut walls and wine bottles, it's a charming spot to recharge your batteries over tea and homemade cake, a light lunch or laid-back dinner. There's also brunch on Sundays. (06 700 87 43; www.cafecafebistrot.it; Via dei Santissimi Quattro Coronati 44; meals €15-20; 9.30am-11pm; Via di San Giovanni in Laterano)

Aroma

RISTORANTE €€€

10 Map p100, B1

One for a special-occasion dinner, the rooftop restaurant of the Palazzo Manfredi hotel offers 'marry-me' views of the Colosseum and Michelin-starred food that rises to the occasion. Overseeing the kitchen is chef Giuseppe Di Iorio, whose brand of luxurious, forward-thinking Mediterranean cuisine has won widespread applause from critics and diners alike. (06 9761 5109; www.aromarestaurant.it; Via Labicana 125; tasting menu €130; 12.30-3pm & 7.30-11.30pm; Via Labicana)

Il Bocconcino

TRATTORIA €€

11 Map p100, B2

One of the better options in the touristy pocket near the Colosseum, this laid-back trattoria stands out for its authentic regional cooking and use of locally sourced seasonal ingredients. Daily specials are chalked up on blackboards or there's a regular menu of classic Roman pastas, meaty mains and imaginative desserts. (06 7707 9175; www.ilbocconcino.com; Via Ostilia 23; meals €35; 12.30-3.30pm & 7.30-11.30pm Thu-Tue, closed Aug; Via Labicana)

Li Rioni

PIZZA €

12 Map p100, B2

Locals swear by Li Rioni, arriving for the second sitting at 9pm after the tourists have left. A classic neighbourhood pizzeria, it buzzes most nights as diners squeeze into the kitschy interior – set up as a Roman street scene – and tuck into wood-fired thin-crust pizzas and crispy fried starters. (☑ 06 7045 0605; Via dei Santissimi Quattro Coronati 24; meals €15-20; ⏰ 7pm-midnight Thu-Tue, closed Aug; 🚇 Via di San Giovanni in Laterano)

Taverna dei Quaranta

TRATTORIA €€

13 🍽 Map p100, B2

Tasty traditional food and a prime location – near the Colosseum but just off the beaten track – are the hallmarks of this family-run trattoria. There are no great surprises on the menu but daily specials add variety and the desserts are homemade – always a good sign. (☑ 06 700 05 50; www.tavernadeiquaranta.com; Via Claudia 24; meals €30; ⏰ noon-3.30pm & 7.30pm-midnight; 🚇 Via Claudia)

Caffè Propaganda

BISTRO €€

14 🍽 Map p100, B2

This Parisian-inspired bistro is a good-looking place with a striking zinc bar, 5m-high ceilings, bric-a-brac on the white-tiled walls, and a menu that covers all the bases, with everything from cocktails and cake to traditional Roman pastas, omelettes, salads and *dolci* (sweets). (☑ 06 9453 4256; www.caffepropaganda.it; Via Claudia 15; meals €30-40; ⏰ 12.30pm-2am Tue-Sun; 🚇 Via Claudia)

Drinking

Il Pentagrappolo

WINE BAR

15 🍷 Map p100, B2

This vaulted, softly lit bar is the perfect antidote to sightseeing overload. Join the mellow crowd for an evening of wine and jazz courtesy of the frequent live gigs. There's also lunch and a daily *aperitivo* (bar buffet). (Via Celimontana 21b; ⏰ noon-3pm & 6pm-1am Tue-Fri, 6pm-1am Sat & Sun; Ⓜ Colosseo)

Coming Out

BAR

16 🍷 Map p100, B1

On warm evenings, with lively crowds on the street and the Colosseum as a

---

STEFANO SCATÀ/IMAGE COURTESY OF CAFFÈ PROPAGANDA ©

Caffè Propaganda

backdrop, there are few finer places to sip than this friendly gay bar. It's open all day but at its best in the evening when the the atmosphere hots up and the gigs, drag shows and karaoke nights get under way. (www.comingout.it; Via di San Giovanni in Laterano 8; ⊙7am-2am; 🚇Via Labicana)

Shopping

Soul Food   MUSIC

17 🔒 Map p100, C2

Run by Hate Records, Soul Food is a laid-back record store with an eclectic collection of vinyl that runs the musical gamut, from '60s garage and rockabilly to punk, indie, new wave, folk, funk and soul. You'll also find retro-design T-shirts, fanzines and other groupie clobber. (www.haterecords. com; Via di San Giovanni in Laterano 192; ⊙10.30am-1.30pm & 3.30-8pm Tue-Sat; 🚇Via di San Giovanni in Laterano)

Via Sannio   MARKET

18 🔒 Map p100, E3

This clothes market in the shadow of the Aurelian Walls is awash with wardrobe staples. It has a good assortment of new and vintage clothes, bargain-price shoes, jeans and leather jackets. (⊙9am-1.30pm Mon-Sat; Ⓜ San Giovanni)

Local Life
Ostiense & San Paolo

Packed with post-industrial grit, Ostiense is all about exuberant street art, cutting-edge clubs and cool bars. The presence of a university campus lends it a buzz and its disused factories provide space for all sorts of after-hours hedonism. Traditional sights are thin on the ground but you'll find a fabulous museum housed in a former power-erplant and the world's third-largest church.

Getting There

Ostiense extends south of the city centre along Via Ostiense.

M Metro Line B runs to Piramide, Garbatella and Basilica San Paolo.

Bus Routes 23 and 716 serve Via Ostiense.

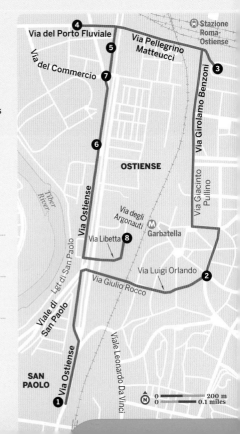

1 Basilica di San Paolo Fuori le Mura

Start your tour at the **Basilica di San Paolo Fuori le Mura** (www.abbaziasanpaolo. net; Via Ostiense 190; cloisters €4, archaeological walk €4, audioguide €5; ⏰7am-6.30pm; Ⓜ San Paolo), the world's third largest church. Much of the original basilica was destroyed by fire in 1823 but a few features have survived, including the 5th-century triumphal arch, with its heavily restored mosaics, and the Gothic tabernacle.

2 Garbatella

To experience one of Rome's most idiosyncratic neighbourhoods, make for **Garbatella** (Ⓜ Garbatella), a colourful garden suburb that was developed in the 1920s and '30s to house people who'd been displaced by fascist construction projects in the city centre.

3 Lunch at Eataly

For lunch, push on to **Eataly** (☎06 9027 9201; www.eataly.net/it_en; Air Terminal Ostiense, Piazzale XII Ottobre 1492; ⏰shop 10am-midnight, restaurants noon-11.30pm; Ⓜ Piramide), a vast foodie complex where you can take your pick of 19 restaurants and cafes.

4 Street Art on Via del Porto Fluviale

Walk off your meal on **Via del Porto Fluviale**, home to some of Rome's most inventive street art. Urban art has really taken off in Rome and Ostiense's abandoned factories boast some impressive murals by the Bolognese artist Blu.

5 Coffee & Cakes at Andreotti

Treat yourself to afternoon coffee and cake at **Andreotti** (☎06 575 07 73; Via Ostiense 54; ⏰7.30am-9.30pm; Ⓜ Via Ostiense). Film director and local resident Ferzan Ozpetek is a fan and has been known to cast its *dolci* (sweets) in his films.

6 Sculpture at Centrale Montemartini

The **Centrale Montemartini** (☎06 06 08; www.centralemontemartini.org; Via Ostiense 106; adult/reduced €7.50/6.50, incl Capitoline Museums €16/14, valid 7 days; ⏰9am-7pm Tue-Sun; Ⓜ Via Ostiense) is the striking southern outpost of the Capitoline Museums. In an ex-powerplant, ancient Roman sculpture is juxtaposed against diesel engines and giant furnaces.

7 Aperitivo at Doppiozeroo

Early evening is *aperitivo* time, and the place to go is **Doppiozeroo** (☎06 5730 1961; www.doppiozeroo.com; Via Ostiense 68; ⏰7am-2am Mon-Sat; Ⓜ Piramide). Between 6pm and 9pm, fashion-conscious Romans flock to this urbane bar to fill up on its famously lavish *aperitivo* buffet.

8 Cool Clubbing

Ostiense is serious clubbing country, where top-notch DJs dish out anything from nu-house to thumping techno. Big clubs include **Goa** (☎06 574 82 77; www.goaclub.com; Via Libetta 13; ⏰11.30pm-4.30am Thu-Sat; Ⓜ Garbatella), **Neo Club** (Via degli Argonauti 18; ⏰11pm-4am Fri & Sat; Ⓜ Garbatella), and **La Saponeria** (☎06 574 69 99; Via degli Argonauti 20; ⏰11pm-4.30am Tue-Sun Oct-May; Ⓜ Garbatella).

Explore

Aventino & Testaccio

Rising above the mighty ruins of the Terme di Caracalla (pictured above), the Aventino (Aventine hill) is a graceful district of villas, lush gardens and austere churches. At the top, Via di Santa Sabina boasts one of Rome's great curiosities – a keyhole view of St Peter's dome. Below, the traditional working-class district of Testaccio is a popular nightlife hang-out and a bastion of classical Roman cuisine.

The Sights in a Day

Start your day with an imaginary workout at the **Terme di Caracalla** (p111), one of ancient Rome's largest baths complexes. Once you're done, push on to Testaccio for a taste of neighbourhood life. Join the locals for a nose around the **Nuovo Mercato di Testaccio** (p115), stop for a coffee at **Linari** (p115) and then grab a takeaway from **Trapizzino** (p113).

See in the afternoon at the **Cimitero Acattolico per gli Stranieri** (p112), the final resting place of poets Keats and Shelley, before hiking up to the Aventino. It's quite a walk but worth it for the remarkable keyhole view from the **Priorato dei Cavalieri di Malta** (p111) and the heart-melting panoramas from **Parco Savello** (p111). While up here, make sure to look into the austere **Basilica di Santa Sabina** (p111).

Spend the evening in Testaccio. Dine on fab Roman fare at **Flavio al Velavevodetto** (p112) and then let your hair down at clubbing favourite **ConteStaccio** (p115).

 Best of Rome

Eating
Flavio al Velavevodetto (p112)

Pizzeria Da Remo (p113)

Trapizzino (p113)

Il Gelato (p113)

Architecture
Terme di Caracalla (p111)

Basilica di Santa Sabina (p111)

Nightlife
ConteStaccio (p115)

Shopping
Volpetti (p115)

Nuovo Mercato di Testaccio (p115)

Culture
Terme di Caracalla (p111)

ConteStaccio (p115)

Getting There

Ⓜ **Metro** For Testaccio take line B to Piramide. The Aventino is walkable from Testaccio and Circo Massimo (line B).

🚍 **Bus** Route 714 serves the Terme di Caracalla from Termini and San Giovanni; bus 715 runs to the Aventino from Via del Teatro di Marcello.

🚋 **Tram** Route 3 runs from San Giovanni along Viale Aventino to Testaccio.

For reviews see

◎ Sights   p111
✕ Eating   p112
🍷 Drinking   p114
★ Entertainment   p115
🛍 Shopping   p115

CAMPITELLI

Parco San Sebastiano

Via di Valle delle Camene

Parco di Valle delle Camene

Terme di Caracalla ◎ 1

Via del San Gregorio

Viale delle Terme di Caracalla

Parco di Porta Capena

Viale Guido Baccelli

Piazza di Santa Balbina

Via Guido

Via di Villa Pepoli

Viale di Villa Pepoli

Via Rosa Raimondi

AVENTINO

Via dei Cerchi

Circo Massimo Ⓜ

Via del Circo Massimo

Via di Santa Prisca

UN Food & Agriculture Organisation (FAO)

Via Aventina

Via Antonina

Via Pennazzi

Viale Aventino ✕ 11

Via Bramante

Roseto Comunale

Via di Fonte di Fauno

Via Terme Deciane

Via di Prisca

Piazza Santa Prisca

Via A Palladio

Via Flaminio Ponzio

Via C Maratta

Via Giotto

Via di Porta Ardeatina

Viale Marco Polo

Clivo de Publicii

Piazza Albania

Parco Savello ◎ 4

Basilica di Santa Sabina ◎ 3

Via di Santa Sabina

Via di San Alessio

Via Melania

Viale della Piramide Cestia

Piramide di Caio Cestio

Piramide Ⓜ

Piazzale Ostiense

Stazione Roma Ostia Ⓡ

Via Ostiense

Priorato dei Cavalieri di Malta ◎ 2

Piazza dei Cavalieri di Malta

Viale M Gelsomini

Porta di Ripa Grande

Lgt Aventino

Via Marmorata 17 🛍

Cimitero Acattolico per gli Stranieri ◎ 5

Via Luca della Robbia

Via di San Michele

Ponte Sublicio

13 🍷

Via Mastro Giorgio

10 ✕

Via Nicola Zabaglia

Via Manuzio

Monte Testaccio

16 🛍

Piazzale Portuense

Tiber River

Lgt Testaccio

Via G.B. Bodoni

Via Branca

Piazza Testaccio

Via Ginori

14 🛍

Via Beniamino Franklin

8 ✕ 🍷

Piazza Santa Maria Liberatrice

9 ✕

Via Vanvitelli

Via Vecellio

TESTACCIO

Via Galvani

7 ✕

MACRO Testaccio ◎ 6

12 ✕ 18 🍷

15 🛍

Piazza Orazio Giustiniani

Via di Monte Testaccio

Via Florio

Via Anicia

Via Portuense

0 ——— 200 m
0 ——— 0.1 miles

Sights

Terme di Caracalla

ARCHAEOLOGICAL SITE

1 Map p110, E3

The remains of the emperor Caracalla's vast baths complex are among Rome's most awe-inspiring ruins. Inaugurated in AD 216, the original 10-hectare site, which comprised baths, gyms, libraries, shops and gardens, was used by up to 8000 people daily. Most of the ruins are what's left of the central bath house. This was a huge rectangular edifice bookended by two **palestre** (gyms) and centred on a **frigidarium** (cold room), where bathers would stop after spells in the warmer **tepidarium** and dome-capped **caldaria** (hot room). (06 3996 7700; www.coopculture.it; Viale delle Terme di Caracalla 52; adult/reduced €6/3; 9am-1hr before sunset Tue-Sun, 9am-2pm Mon; Viale delle Terme di Caracalla)

Priorato dei Cavalieri di Malta

HISTORIC BUILDING

2 Map p110, B1

Fronting an ornate cypress-shaded piazza, the Roman headquarters of the Cavalieri di Malta (Knights of Malta) boast one of Rome's most celebrated views. It's not immediately apparent but look through the keyhole in the Priorato's green door and you'll see the dome of St Peter's Basilica perfectly aligned at the end of a hedge-lined avenue. (Piazza dei Cavalieri di Malta; closed to the public; Lungotevere Aventino)

Top Tip

Opera & Ballet at the Terme di Caracalla

Between June and August, the Terme di Caracalla hosts a summer season of opera and ballet. Check www.operaroma.it for details.

Basilica di Santa Sabina

BASILICA

3 Map p110, C1

This solemn basilica, one of Rome's most beautiful medieval churches, was founded by Peter of Illyria in around AD 422. It was enlarged in the 9th century and again in 1216, just before it was given to the newly founded Dominican order – note the tombstone of Muñoz de Zamora, one of the order's founding fathers, in the nave floor. A 20th-century restoration returned it to its original look. (06 5 79 41; Piazza Pietro d'Illiria 1; 6.30am-12.45pm & 3-8pm; Lungotevere Aventino)

Parco Savello

PARK

4 Map p110, C1

Known to Romans as the Giardino degli Aranci (Orange Garden), this pocket-sized park is a romantic haven. Grab a perch at the small panoramic terrace and watch the sun set over the Tiber and St Peter's dome. (Via di Santa Sabina; 7am-6pm Oct-Feb, to 8pm Mar & Sep, to 9pm Apr-Aug; Lungotevere Aventino)

Cimitero Acattolico per gli Stranieri

CEMETERY

5 ⦿ Map p110, B4

Despite the roads that surround it, Rome's 'non-Catholic' Cemetery is a verdant oasis of peace. An air of Grand Tour romance hangs over the site where up 4000 people lie buried, including poets Keats and Shelley, and Italian political thinker Antonio Gramsci. Among the gravestones and cypress trees look out for the *Angelo del Dolore* (Angel of Grief), a much-replicated 1894 sculpture that US artist William Wetmore Story created for his wife's grave. (www. cemeteryrome.it; Via Caio Cestio 5; voluntary donation €3; ⏱9am-5pm Mon-Sat, to 1pm Sun; Ⓜ️Piramide)

🔍 Local Life

Monte Testaccio

Get to the heart of the local landscape at **Monte Testaccio** (☑06 06 08; Via Nicolo Zabaglia 24, cnr Via Galvani; adult/reduced €4/3, plus cost of tour; ⏱group visits only, reservation necessary; 🚊Via Marmorata), a 49m-high artificial hill. Between the 2nd century BC and the 3rd century AD, Testaccio was Rome's river port. Supplies of olive oil were transported here in huge terracotta amphorae, which, once emptied, were broken and the fragments stacked in a huge pile near the storehouses. Over time, this pile grew into a hill – Monte Testaccio.

MACRO Testaccio

GALLERY

6 ⦿ Map p110, A4

Housed in Rome's former slaughterhouse, MACRO Testaccio (the second of the Museo d'Arte Contemporanea di Roma's two exhibition spaces) is part of a cultural complex that also includes Rome's Accademia di Belle Arti and the University of Roma Tre's Architecture Faculty. Contemporary art exhibitions are staged in two cavernous industrial halls. Visitors should note that the gallery opens only when there's an exhibition on – check the website for details. (☑06 06 08; www.museomacro.org; Piazza Orazio Giustiniani 4; adult/reduced €8.50/7.50; ⏱4-10pm Tue-Sun; 🚊Via Marmorata)

Eating

Flavio al Velavevodetto

TRATTORIA €€

7 🍴 Map p110, B3

Housed in a rustic Pompeian-red villa, this welcoming eatery specialises in earthy, no-nonsense *cucina romana* (Roman cuisine). Expect antipasti of cheeses and cured meats, huge helpings of homemade pastas, and uncomplicated meat dishes. (☑06 574 41 94; www.ristorantevelavevo detto.it; Via di Monte Testaccio 97-99; meals €30-35; ⏱12.30-3pm & 7.45-11pm; 🚊Via Galvani)

Pizzeria Da Remo

PIZZA €

8 🍴 Map p110, A2

For an authentic Roman experience, join the noisy crowds at this, one of the city's best-known and most popular pizzerias. It's a spartan-looking place, but the thin-crust Roman pizzas are the business, and there's a cheerful, boisterous vibe. Expect to queue after 8.30pm. (📞06 574 62 70; Piazza Santa Maria Liberatrice 44; pizzas from €5.50; ⏰7pm-1am Mon-Sat; 🚇Via Marmorata)

Trapizzino

FAST FOOD €

9 🍴 Map p110, A3

This pocket-size joint is the birthplace of the *trapizzino,* a kind of hybrid sandwich made by stuffing a small cone of doughy bread with fillers such as *polpette al sugo* (meatballs in tomato sauce) or *pollo alla cacciatore* (stewed chicken). They're messy to eat but quite delicious. (www.trapizzino.it; Via Branca 88; trapizzini from €3.50; ⏰noon-1am Tue-Sun; 🚇Via Marmorata)

Da Felice

LAZIO CUISINE €€

10 🍴 Map p110, B3

Foodies swear by this historic stalwart, famous for its unwavering dedication to local culinary traditions. In contrast to the light-touch modern decor, the menu is pure old-school with a classic weekly timetable: *pasta e fagioli* (pasta and beans) on Tuesdays, *bollito di manzo* (boiled beef) on Thursdays, seafood on

RICHARD GOERG/GETTY IMAGES ©

Angelo del Dolore, Cimitero Acattolico

Fridays. Reservations essential. (📞06 574 68 00; www.feliceatestaccio.it; Via Mastro Giorgio 29; meals €35-40; ⏰12.30-3pm & 7.30-10.30pm; 🚇Via Marmorata)

Il Gelato

GELATERIA €

11 🍴 Map p110, D2

This is the Aventine outpost of the gelato empire built by Rome's ice-cream king, Claudio Torcè. His creamy creations are seasonal and preservative free, ranging from the classic to the decidedly not – anyone for salted peanut or green tea? (Viale Aventino 59; gelato €2-4.50; ⏰10am-midnight summer, 11am-9pm winter; 🚇Viale Aventino)

Checchino dal 1887

LAZIO CUISINE €€€

12 🍴 📍 Map p110, A4

A pig's whisker from the city's former slaughterhouse, Checchino is one of the grander restaurants specialising in the *quinto quarto* (fifth quarter – or insides of the animal). Signature dishes include *coda all vaccinara* (oxtail stew) and *rigatoni alla pajata* (pasta tubes with a sauce of tomato and veal intestines). (☎06 574 63 18; www.checchino-dal-1887.com; Via di Monte Testaccio 30; tasting menus €40-65; ⏱12.30-3pm & 8pm-midnight Tue-Sat; 🚇Via Galvani)

Drinking

Rec 23

BAR

13 🍸 📍 Map p110, B2

All plate glass and exposed brick, this popular, NY-inspired venue caters to all moods, serving *aperitivo*, restaurant meals, and a weekend brunch. Arrive thirsty to take on the Testaccio Mule, one of a long list of cocktails, or get to grips with the selection of Scottish whiskies and Latin American rums. (☎06 8746 2147; www.rec23.com; Piazza dell'Emporio 2; ⏱6.30pm-2am daily & 12.30-3.30pm Sat & Sun; 🚇Via Marmorata)

Understand
Roman Cuisine

Like many Italian regional cuisines, classic Roman cooking was born out of poverty and the judicious use of seasonal, local ingredients.

Offal
One of the trademarks of true Roman cuisine is offal, the so-called *quinto quarto* (fifth quarter). This taste for nose-to-tail eating arose in Testaccio around the city abattoir, and still today *pajata* (veal intestines), *trippa* (tripe) and *coda alla vaccinara* (oxtail stew) are prized city staples.

Roman-Jewish Food
Much Roman cuisine is Jewish in origin, based on dishes that the city's Jewish community developed during centuries of confinement in the ghetto. Two dishes stand out: *carciofi alla giudia* (deep-fried artichoke) and *fiori di zucca fritti* (fried courgette flowers stuffed with mozzarella and anchovies).

Signature Dishes
Other iconic Roman dishes include *spaghetti alla carbonara* (with egg, cheese and *guanciale* bacon), *bucatini all'amatriciana* (thick spaghetti with tomato sauce and *guanciale*), *cacio e pepe* (pasta with pecorino cheese and pepper) and *saltimbocca* (veal cutlet with ham and sage).

Linari
CAFE

14 Map p110, A3

A local hang-out, Linari has the busy clatter of a good bar, with excellent pastries, splendid coffee and plenty of barside banter. There are a few outside tables, ideal for a cheap lunch, but you'll have to outfox the neighbourhood ladies to get one. (Via Nicola Zabaglia 9; 🕑7am-11pm Wed-Mon; 🚊Via Marmorata)

L'Alibi
CLUB

15 Map p110, A4

A historic gay club, L'Alibi does high-camp with style, putting on kitsch shows and playing house, techno and dance to a mixed gay and straight crowd. If the sweaty atmosphere on the dance floors gets too much, head up to the spacious summer terrace. Saturday's Tommy Night is the hot date right now. (Via di Monte Testaccio 44; 🕑11.30pm-5am Thu-Sun; 🚊Via Galvani)

Entertainment

ConteStaccio
LIVE MUSIC

16 Map p110, B4

With an under-the-stars terrace and cool, arched interior, ConteStaccio is something of a multipurpose outfit with a cocktail bar, pizzeria and restaurant, but is best known for its daily concerts. Gigs span indie, rock, acoustic, funk and electronic. (www.contestaccio. com; Via di Monte Testaccio 65b; 🕑7pm-4am Tue-Sun; 🚊Via Galvani)

Top Tip

Clubbing Notes

Clubs tend to get busy after midnight, or even after 2am. Often admission is free, but drinks are expensive. Note also that it pays to dress up if you want to get in.

Shopping

Volpetti
FOOD & DRINK

17 Map p110, B3

This superstocked deli, considered by many the best in town, is a treasure trove of gourmet delicacies. Helpful staff will guide you through the extensive selection of smelly cheeses, homemade pastas, olive oils, vinegars, cured meats, vegie pies, wines and grappas. It also serves excellent sliced pizza. (www. volpetti.com; Via Marmorata 47; 🕑8am-2pm & 5-8.15pm Mon-Sat; 🚊Via Marmorata)

Nuovo Mercato di Testaccio
MARKET

18 Map p110, A3

Even if you don't need to buy anything, a trip to Testaccio's daily food market is fun. Occupying a modern, purpose-built site, it hums with activity as locals go about their daily shopping, picking, prodding and sniffing the brightly coloured produce and cheerfully shouting at all and sundry. (entrances Via Galvani, Via Beniamino Franklin; 🕑6am-3pm Mon-Sat; 🚊Via Marmorata)

Explore

Trastevere & Gianicolo

Trastevere, with its cobbled lanes and ochre *palazzi* (mansions), is one of Rome's best-looking and most vivacious neighbourhoods. Formerly a bastion of working-class independence, it's now a trendy hang-out full of restaurants, cafes and pubs catering to a colourful cast of tourists, travellers, students and street sellers. Behind it, the Gianicolo hill rises serenely above the maelstrom, offering superb views.

TIM WHITE/GETTY IMAGES ©

The Sights in a Day

Start the day by paying homage to St Cecilia, the patron saint of music, at the **Basilica di Santa Cecilia in Trastevere** (p123), and then spying on a saucy Bernini sculpture at the **Chiesa di San Francesco d'Assisi a Ripa** (p123). Suitably inspired, head over to Piazza Santa Maria in Trastevere and the neighbourhood's main must-see, the **Basilica di Santa Maria in Trastevere** (p118). For a final flourish before lunch, continue on to **Villa Farnesina** (p123), a palatial Renaissance villa famed for its Raphael frescoes.

After lunch at **Pianostrada Laboratorio di Cucina** (p125), retrace your footsteps back to the **Galleria Nazionale d'Arte Antica di Palazzo Corsini** (p124). Afterwards, take an hour or so to chill out in the nearby **Orto Botanico** (p124). Recharged, head up the Gianicolo hill to admire Bramante's **Tempietto** (p123) and some superb rooftop views.

For a real Trastevere night to remember, dine at **Glass Hostaria** (p125) and then try the neighbourhood's best beer at **Ma Che Siete Venuti a Fà** (p126).

For a local's night out in Trastevere and Gianicolo, see p120.

 Top Sights

Basilica di Santa Maria in Trastevere (p118)

Local Life

A Night Out in Trastevere & Gianicolo (p120)

Best of Rome

Culture
Big Mama (p121)

Lettere Caffè Gallery (p127)

Nuovo Sacher (p121)

Architecture
Tempietto di Bramante (p123)

Eating
Glass Hostaria (p125)

Getting There

Tram Route 8 runs from the *centro storico* (historic centre) to Viale di Trastevere. Tram 3 also stops at the southern end of Viale Trastevere, and connects with Testaccio, Colosseo, San Giovanni and Villa Borghese.

Bus From Termini, bus H runs to Viale di Trastevere. For Gianicolo, take bus 870 from Piazza delle Rovere.

Top Sights
Basilica di Santa Maria in Trastevere

This glittering basilica is said to be the oldest church in Rome dedicated to the Virgin Mary. Dating to the early 3rd century, it was commissioned by Pope Callixtus III on the site where, according to legend, a fountain of oil had miraculously sprung from the ground. The basilica has been much altered over the centuries and its current Romanesque form is the result of a 12th-century revamp. The portico came later, added by Carlo Fontana in 1702.

⊙ Map p122, B3

Piazza Santa Maria in Trastevere

⊙ 7.30am-9pm

🚊 Viale di Trastevere, 🚊 Viale di Trastevere

Mosaics in the Basilica di Santa Maria in Trastevere

Don't Miss

The Exterior

Rising above the four papal statues on Carlo Fontana's 18th-century porch, the basilica's restrained 12th-century facade is most notable for its beautiful medieval mosaic. This glittering gold banner depicts Mary feeding Jesus surrounded by 10 women bearing lamps.

Towering above the church is a 12th-century Romanesque bell tower, complete with its very own mosaic – look in the small niche near the top.

The Mosaics

The basilica's main drawcard is its golden 12th-century mosaics. In the apse, look out for the dazzling depiction of Christ and his mother flanked by various saints, and, on the far left, Pope Innocent II holding a model of the church. Beneath this is a series of six mosaics by Pietro Cavallini (c 1291) illustrating the life of the Virgin.

Interior Design

The interior boasts a typical 12th-century design with three naves divided by 21 Roman columns, some plundered from the Terme di Caracalla. On the right of the altar, near a spiralling Paschal candlestick, is an inscription, 'Fons Olei', which marks the spot where the miraculous oil fountain supposedly sprung. Up above, the coffered golden ceiling was designed by Domenichino in 1617.

Cappella Avila

The last chapel on the left, the Cappella Avila, is worth a look for its stunning 17th-century dome. Antonio Gherardi's clever 1680 design depicts four angels holding the circular base of a large lantern whose columns rise to give the effect of a second cupola within a larger outer dome.

JEAN-PIERRE LESCOURRET/GETTY IMAGES ©

☑ Top Tips

▶ Have some coins handy to drop in the light box to illuminate the mosaics.

▶ Avoid visiting during mass, which is held at 9am, 5.30pm and 8.30pm Monday to Friday; 9am, 5.30pm and 8pm Saturday; 8.30am, 10am, 11.30am, 5.30pm and 6.45pm Sunday. Services are cut back in July and August.

▶ To see the facade in its entirety, step back so you can see above the porch.

✗ Take a Break

Avoid the rip-off tourist traps on the piazza outside. Instead, grab a drink or snack at Ombre Rosse (p126), ideally at one of its street-side tables. Alternatively, enjoy a tasty meal from the hit foodie hot spot Pianostrada Laboratorio di Cucina (p125).

Local Life
A Night Out in Trastevere & Gianicolo

With its enchanting lanes, vibrant piazzas and carnival atmosphere, Trastevere is one of the city's favourite after-dark hang-outs. Foreigners love it, but it's also a local haunt and Romans come here in swaths, particularly on balmy summer nights when street sellers set up camp on the picturesque alleyways and bar crowds spill out onto the streets.

1 Views on the Gianicolo

The early evening is a good time to enjoy sweeping panoramic views from the Gianicolo, Rome's highest, was the scene of vicious fighting during Italian unification but is now a tranquil, romantic spot. Lap up the vibe with a drink from **Bar Stuzzichini** (Piazzale Giuseppe Garibaldi; ⏰7.30am-1am or 2am; 🚌Passeggiata del Gianicolo) on Piazzale Giuseppe Garibaldi.

2 Aperitivo at Freni e Frizioni

Once back down in the fray, head to **Freni e Frizioni** (📞06 4549 7499; www.frenifrizioni.com; Via del Politeama 4-6; ⏱6.30pm-2am; �Piazza Trilussa) for an *aperitivo* (bar buffet). This perennially cool bar pulls in a spritz-loving young crowd that swells onto the small piazza outside to sip cocktails (from €7) and fill up at the bar buffet (€6 to €10, 7pm to 10pm).

3 Dinner at Da Olindo

For a real Trastevere dining experience, **Da Olindo** (📞06 581 88 35; Vicolo della Scala 8; meals €25; ⏱7.30-11pm Mon-Sat; 🚊Viale di Trastevere) is classic family affair. With its lively atmosphere and robust, no-nonsense cooking, it's an authentic spot to try traditional dishes such as *coniglio all cacciatore* (rabbit, hunter-style) or *polpette al sugo* (meatballs in sauce).

4 Hanging Out on Piazza Santa Maria in Trastevere

Trastevere's focal square, **Piazza Santa Maria in Trastevere** (🚊Viale di Trastevere, 🚊Viale di Trastevere), is a prime people-watching spot. During the day it's full of chatting locals and guidebook-toting tourists but by night the foreign students, young Romans and out-of-towners move in, all on the lookout for a good time. The octagonal fountain is of Roman origin and was restored by Carlo Fontana in 1692.

5 Chocolate at Bar San Calisto

Those in the know head to **Bar San Calisto** (📞06 589 56 78; Piazza San Calisto 3-5; ⏱6am-1.45am Mon-Sat; 🚊Viale di Trastevere, 🚊Viale di Trastevere), a down-at-heel institution popular with everyone from intellectuals to keeping-it-real Romans, alcoholics and American students. It's famous for its chocolate – hot with cream in winter, with gelato in summer.

6 Catch a film at Nuovo Sacher

Join Rome's passionate cinephiles at the **Nuovo Sacher** (📞06 581 81 16; www.sacherfilm.eu; Largo Ascianghi 1; 🚊Viale di Trastevere, 🚊Viale di Trastevere), a small cinema owned by cult Roman director Nanni Moretti. A well-known venue for film-related events, it's the perfect place to catch the latest European art-house offering, with films regularly screened in their original language.

7 Blues at Big Mama

To wallow in the Eternal City blues, there's only one place to go – **Big Mama** (📞06 581 25 51; www.bigmama.it; Vicolo di San Francesco a Ripa 18; ⏱9pm-1.30am, shows 10.30pm, closed Jun-Sep; 🚊Viale di Trastevere, 🚊Viale di Trastevere), a cramped Trastevere basement. There are weekly residencies from well-known Italian musicians, and frequent blues, jazz, funk, soul and R&B concerts by international artists.

A **B** **C** **D**

Via dei Riari

Via della Lungara

Lgt della Farnesina

Villa Farnesina

5 6

Galleria Nazionale d'Arte Antica di Palazzo Corsini

6 Orto Botanico

Gianicolo (Janiculum)

Via Garibaldi

Via dei Matthiato

Via della Scala

Piazza della Scala

27 16

10 Piazza Sant'Egidio

GIANICOLO
Piazza San Pietro in Montorio

3 Tempietto di Bramante & Chiesa di San Pietro in Montorio

20 18

Via Calandrelli

Via Sacchi

Via Marneli

Via della Paglia

Via G Venzian

Via Luciano Manara

Basilica di Santa Maria in Trastevere

Santa Maria in Trastevere

11 Piazza San Calisto

13

Piazza San Cosimato

8

Via Morosini

Via F Casini

Viale Glorioso

Via Dandolo

Via Dandolo

Viale di Trastevere

Largo Ascianghi

Piazza Bernardino da Feltre

Tiber River

Lgt dei Tebaldi

Via Giulia

Ponte Sisto

Via Corsini

15 25 Piazza Trillussa

Via Benedetta

Via del Bologna

19

Vic del Cinque

Via del Moro

9 17 Via della Pelliccia

14

Via delle Pettinari

Via delle Zoccolette

Lgt dei Vallati

Lgt Raphaello Sanzio

Ponte Garibaldi

Via Renella

Via della Lungaretta

23

Via dei Fienaroli

Via di San Gallicano

Via San Francesco a Ripa

24

Piazza Mastai

TRASTEVERE

Via della Luce

21 2 Chiesa di San Francesco d'Assisi a Ripa

Piazza di San Francesco d'Assisi

Largo Ascianghi

22 Piazzale Portuense

Via Portuense

Lgt de Cenci

Ponte Tiberina

Isola Tiberina

Lgt degli Anguillara

Piazza Belli

7

Piazza Sonnino

Piazza in Piscinula

Via dei Salumi

Via G C Santini

Via dei Genovesi

12

Basilica di Santa Cecilia in Trastevere

1 26 Piazza di Santa Cecilia

Via della Madonna dell'Orio

Piazza de' Mercanti

Via Anicia

Via di San Michele

Porta di Ripa Grande

Piazza Porta Portese

Ponte Sublicio

Lgt Aventino

For reviews see	
Top Sights	p118
Sights	p123
Eating	p124
Drinking	p126
Entertainment	p127
Shopping	p128

0 — 200 m
0 — 0.1 miles

Sights

Basilica di Santa Cecilia in Trastevere
BASILICA

1 Map p122, D4

The last resting place of the patron saint of music features Pietro Cavallini's stunning 13th-century fresco in the nuns' choir. Inside the church itself, Stefano Maderno's mysterious sculpture depicts St Cecilia's miraculously preserved body, unearthed in the Catacombs of San Callisto in 1599. You can also visit the excavations of Roman houses, one of which was possibly that of Cecilia. (Piazza di Santa Cecilia; fresco & crypt each €2.50; ⊘basilica & crypt 9.30am-1pm & 4-7.15pm, fresco 10am-2.30pm Mon-Sat; 🚊Viale di Trastevere, 🚋Viale di Trastevere)

Chiesa di San Francesco d'Assisi a Ripa
CHURCH

2 Map p122, C4

St Francis is said to have stayed here in the 13th century, and you can still see the rock that he used as a pillow and his crucifix in his cell. Rebuilt several times, the church's current incarnation dates from the 1680s. It contains one of Bernini's most daring works, the *Beata Ludovica Albertoni* (Blessed Ludovica Albertoni; 1674), a work of highly charged sexual ambiguity. (Piazza di San Francesco d'Assisi 88; ⊘7.30am-noon & 2-7.30pm; 🚊Viale di Trastevere, 🚋Viale di Trastevere)

Tempietto di Bramante & Chiesa di San Pietro in Montorio
CHURCH

3 Map p122, A3

Considered the first great building of the High Renaissance, Bramante's sublime Tempietto (Little Temple; 1508) is a perfect surprise, squeezed into the courtyard of the Chiesa di San Pietro in Montorio, on the spot where St Peter is said to have been crucified. It's small, but perfectly formed; its classically inspired design and ideal proportions epitomise the Renaissance zeitgeist. (www.sanpietroinmontorio.it; Piazza San Pietro in Montorio 2; ⊘Chiesa 8.30am-noon & 3-4pm Mon-Fri, Tempietto 9.30am-12.30pm & 2-4.30pm Tue-Fri, 9am-3pm Sat; 🚊Via Garibaldi)

Villa Farnesina
HISTORIC BUILDING

4 Map p122, A1

This gorgeous 16th-century villa's interior is fantastically frescoed from top to bottom. Several paintings in the Loggia of Cupid and Psyche and the Loggia of Galatea, on the ground floor, are attributed to Raphael. On the 1st floor, Peruzzi's dazzling frescoes in the Salone delle Prospettive are a superb illusionary perspective of a colonnade and panorama of 16th-century Rome. (☏06 6802 7268; www.villafarnesina.it; Via della Lungara 230; adult/reduced €6/5; ⊘9am-2pm daily, to 5pm 2nd Sun of month; 🚊Lgt della Farnesina, 🚋Viale di Trastevere)

Festa de' Noantri

July is a good time to visit Trastevere. In the last two weeks of the month, the neighbourhood holds the Festa de' Noantri, a raucous street party to celebrate the district's roots. Events, which are centred on Piazza Santa Maria in Trastevere, kick off with a religious procession and continue with much eating, drinking, dancing and praying.

Galleria Nazionale d'Arte Antica di Palazzo Corsini

GALLERY

5 ◉ Map p122, A1

Once home to Queen Christina of Sweden, whose richly frescoed bedroom witnessed a steady stream of male and female lovers, 16th-century Palazzo Corsini was designed by Ferdinando Fuga, and houses part of Italy's national art collection. The highlights include Caravaggio's mesmerising *San Giovanni Battista* (St John the Baptist), Guido Reni's unnerving *Salome con la Testa di San Giovanni Battista* (Salome with the Head of John the Baptist) and Fra Angelico's Corsini Triptych. (☏06 6880 2323; www.galleria-corsini.beniculturali.it; Via della Lungara 10; adult/reduced €5/2.50, incl Palazzo Barberini €9/4.50; ⏰8.30am-7.30pm Wed-Mon; 🚋Lgt della Farnesina, 🚋Viale di Trastevere)

Orto Botanico

GARDENS

6 ◉ Map p122, A2

Formerly the private grounds of Palazzo Corsini, Rome's 12-hectare botanical gardens are a little-known, slightly neglected-feeling gem and a great place to unwind in a tree-shaded expanse covering the steep slopes of the Gianicolo, though the admission charge is unfortunately also a bit steep. Plants have been cultivated here since the 13th century. (☏06 499 17 107; Largo Cristina di Svezia 24; adult/reduced €8/4; ⏰9am-6.30pm Mon-Sat Apr-Oct, to 5.30pm Nov-Mar; 🚋Lungotevere della Farnesina, Piazza Trilussa)

Eating

La Gensola

SICILIAN €€

7 ✗ Map p122, D3

This tranquil, classy yet unpretentious trattoria thrills foodies with delicious food that has a Sicilian slant and emphasis on seafood, including an excellent tuna tartare, linguine with fresh anchovies and divine *zuccherini* (tiny fish) with fresh mint. (☏06 581 63 12; Piazza della Gensola 15; meals €45; ⏰12.30-3pm & 7.30-11.30pm, closed Sun mid-Jun–mid-Sep; 🚋Viale di Trastevere, 🚋Viale di Trastevere)

Fatamorgana – Trastevere

GELATERIA €

8 ✗ Map p122, B4

One of several Fatamorgana outlets across Rome, this is one of the finest among the city's gourmet gelatarie.

Quality natural ingredients are used to produce creative flavour combos such as pineapple and ginger or pear and gorgonzola. Gluten free. (Via Roma Libera 11, Piazza San Cosimato; cones & tubs from €2; ⏲noon-midnight summer, to 10.30pm winter; 🚇Viale di Trastevere, 🚊Viale di Trastevere)

Glass Hostaria ITALIAN €€€

 9 Map p122, B2

Trastevere's foremost foodie address, the Glass is a modernist-styled, sophisticated setting decorated in warm wood and contemporary gold, with fabulous cooking to match. Chef Cristina Bowerman creates inventive, delicate dishes that combine with fresh ingredients and traditional elements to delight and surprise the palate. There are tasting menus at €75, €80 and €100. (☎06 5833 5903; Vicolo del Cinque 58; meals €90; ⏲7.30-11.30pm Tue-Sun; 🚇Piazza Trilussa)

Pianostrada Laboratorio di Cucina ITALIAN €

10 Map p122, B2

A diminutive, tucked-away place, this all-female-run foodie stop has been attracting attention with its delicious meals such as parmigiana with aubergine and pumpkin, meatballs, burgers, pasta with swordfish and wild fennel, and gourmet sandwiches. It's all exquisitely made and conceived, so squeeze in along the bar or take one of the tiny tables with bar stools. (Vicolo del Cedro; meals €25; ⏲1-4pm & 7.30-11.30pm Tue-Sun; 🚇Piazza Trilussa)

Paris RISTORANTE €€€

11 Map p122, B3

An old-school restaurant set in a 17th-century building with tables on a small piazza, Paris – named for its founder, not the French capital – is the best place outside the Ghetto to sample Roman-Jewish cuisine. Signature dishes include *gran fritto vegetale con baccalà* (deep-fried vegetables with salt cod) and *carciofi alla giudia* (fried artichoke). (☎06 581 53 78; www.ristoranteparis.it; Piazza San Calisto 7a; meals €45-55; ⏲7.30-11pm Mon, 12.30-3pm & 7.30-11pm Tue-Sun; 🚇Viale di Trastevere, 🚊Viale di Trastevere)

Le Mani in Pasta RISTORANTE €€

12 Map p122, D3

Popular and lively, this rustic, snug place has arched ceilings and an open kitchen that serves up delicious fresh pasta dishes such as *fettucine con ricotta e pancetta*. The grilled meats are great, too. (☎06 581 60 17; Via dei Genovesi 37; meals €35; ⏲12.30-3pm & 7.30-11pm Tue-Sun; 🚇Viale di Trastevere, 🚊Viale di Trastevere)

Pizzeria Ivo PIZZA €

 13 Map p122, B3

One of Trastevere's most famous pizzerias, Ivo's has been slinging pizzas for some 40 years, and still the hungry come. With the TV on in the corner and the tables full (a few outside on the cobbled street), Ivo is a noisy and vibrant place, and the waiters fit the gruff-and-fast stereotype. (☎06 581 70 82;

Via di San Francesco a Ripa 158; pizzas from €7; ⏰7pm-midnight Wed-Mon; 🚇Viale di Trastevere, 🚋Viale di Trastevere)

Da Corrado
TRATTORIA €

14 Map p122, B2

Don't expect refined service or a fancy interior. This is a proper Roman old-school trattoria, with no outdoor seating, but an unfussy, rough-and-ready atmosphere. It's packed with locals, feasting on hearty Roman soul food, such as *amatriciana* (pasta with bacon and tomato sauce). (Via della Pelliccia 39; meals €25; ⏰12.30-2.30pm & 7-11pm Mon-Sat; 🚇Viale di Trastevere, 🚋Viale di Trastevere)

Drinking

Ma Che Siete Venuti a Fà
PUB

15 Map p122, B2

Named after a football chant, which translates politely as 'What did you come here for?', this pint-sized Trastevere pub is a beer-buff's paradise, packing in at least 13 international craft beers on tap and even more by the bottle. (www.football-pub.com; Via Benedetta 25; ⏰11am-2am; 🚋Piazza Trilussa)

Da Biagio
WINE BAR

16 Map p122, B2

With the sign 'Vini & Olio' scrawled above the door, this is a hole-in-the-wall Trastevere institution, lined by bottles of grappa and wine-for-sale, but also offering wine and spirits by

the glass, shots and beer on tap. The owner is a funny guy, and has been serving up tipples since 1972. In the evening, drinkers spill out on the cobbled Trastevere street. (www.dabiagio.it; Via della Scala 64; ⏰10am-1.30pm & 5pm-midnight; 🚇Piazza Sonnino)

Ombre Rosse
BAR

17 Map p122, B2

A seminal Trastevere hang-out; grab a table on the terrace and watch the world go by amid a clientele ranging from elderly Italian wide boys to wide-eyed tourists. Tunes are slinky and there's live music (jazz, blues, world) on Thursday evenings from September to April. (☎06 588 41 55; Piazza Sant'Egidio 12; ⏰8am-2am Mon-Sat, 11am-2am Sun; 🚇Piazza Trilussa)

Big Star
BAR

18 Map p122, A4

Off the beaten Trastevere track, this is a cool backstreet bar with an alternative feel and the drink prices scrawled up on a blackboard. It's a small yet airy interior, where you can drink a wide range of beers and cocktails while listening to the hipster DJs, with a laid-back, appealing vibe. (Via Goffredo Mameli 25; ⏰6pm-2am; 🚇Viale de Trastevere, 🚋Viale de Trastevere)

La Mescita
WINE BAR

19 Map p122, B2

This tiny bar inside the entrance to upmarket restaurant Enoteca Ferrara serves delectable *aperitivo* and has a

GLENN BEANLAND/GETTY IMAGES ©

Street scene in Trastevere

wide range of wines by the glass, from €7. Fancy an intimate tête-à-tête, with fine wines and yummy snacks? This is your place. (📞06 5833 3920; Piazza Trilussa 41; 🕐5pm-midnight Sun-Thu, to 1am Fri & Sat; 🚌Piazza Trilussa)

Il Barretto
BAR

20 🚇 Map p122, A3

Venture a little way up the Gianicolo, up a steep flight of steps from Trastevere. Go on, it's worth it: you'll discover this well-kept-secret cocktail bar. The basslines are meaty, the bar staff hip, and the interior mixes vintage with pop art. (📞06 5836 5422; Via Garibaldi 27; 🕐6am-2am Mon-Sat, 5pm-2am Sun; 🚌Piazza Sonnino, 🚊Piazza Sonnino)

Entertainment

Lettere Caffè Gallery
LIVE MUSIC

21 ⭐ Map p122, C4

Like books? Poetry? Blues and jazz? Then you'll love this place – a clutter of bar stools and books, where there are regular live gigs, poetry slams, comedy and gay nights, plus DJ sets playing indie and new wave. (📞06 9727 0991; www.letterecaffe.org; Vicolo di San Francesco a Ripa 100/101; 🕐7pm-2am, closed mid-Aug–mid-Sep; 🚌Viale di Trastevere, 🚊Viale di Trastevere)

Shopping

Porta Portese Market   MARKET

22 Map p122, C5

To see another side of Rome, head to this mammoth flea market. With thousands of stalls selling everything from rare books and fell-off-a-lorry bikes to Peruvian shawls and MP3 players, it's crazily busy and a lot of fun. Keep your valuables safe and wear your haggling hat. (Piazza Porta Portese; ⏱6am-2pm Sun; 🚋Viale di Trastevere, 🚋Viale di Trastevere)

Roma-Store   BEAUTY

23 🔒 Map p122, C3

An enchanting perfume shop crammed full of deliciously enticing bottles of scent, including lots of small, lesser-known brands that will have perfume lovers practically fainting with joy. (☎06 581 87 89; Via della Lungaretta 63; ⏱10am-8pm; 🚋Viale di Trastevere, 🚋Viale di Trastevere)

Antica Caciara Trasteverina   FOOD, WINE

24 🔒 Map p122, C4

The fresh ricotta is prized at this century-old deli, and usually snapped up by lunch. If you're too late, take solace in the famous *pecorino romano* or the *burrata pugliese* (a creamy cheese from the Puglia region), or simply lust after the fragrant hams, bread, Sicilian anchovies and local wines. (Via San Francesco a Ripa 140; ⏱7am-2pm & 4-8pm Mon-Sat; 🚋Viale di Trastevere, 🚋Viale di Trastevere)

Officina della Carta   GIFTS

25 🔒 Map p122, B2

A perfect present pit stop, this tiny workshop produces attractive hand-painted paper-bound boxes, photo albums, recipe books, notepads, photo frames and diaries. (☎06 589 55 57; Via Benedetta 26b; ⏱10.30am-7.30pm Mon-Sat; 🚋Piazza Trilussa)

La Cravatta su Misura   ACCESSORIES

26 🔒 Map p122, D4

With ties draped over the wooden furniture, this inviting shop resembles the study of an absent-minded professor. But don't be fooled: these guys know their ties. Only the finest Italian silks and English wools are used in neckwear made to customers' specifications. At a push, a tie can be ready in a few hours. (☎06 890 69 41; Via di Santa Cecilia 12; ⏱10am-7pm Mon-Sat; 🚋Viale di Trastevere, 🚋Viale di Trastevere)

Scala Quattordici Clothing   CLOTHING

27 🔒 Map p122, B2

Make yourself over à la Audrey Hepburn with these classically tailored clothes in beautiful fabrics – either made-to-measure or off-the-peg. Pricey (a frock will set you back €600 plus) but oh so worth it. (Villa della Scala 13-14; ⏱10am-1.30pm & 4-8pm Tue-Sat, 4-8pm Mon; 🚋Piazza Trilussa)

Understand

Aperitivo

- -

Hit many of the capital's bars in the early evening and you'll find crowds of animated Romans chatting over cocktails and plates of finger food. Welcome to *l'ora d'aperitivo* – happy hour, Roman-style. The *aperitivo*, a nightly ritual imported from the northern cities of Milan and Turin, is basically a souped-up bar buffet served between about 6pm and 9pm. The way it works is that you order your drink – there's usually a standard charge of about €6 to €10 – and tuck into the buffet. Simple.

Classic Drinks

Most bars offer a decent selection of Italian wines and a limited choice of cocktails. But for a classic *aperitivo* tipple you should go for a Negroni, made with Campari, red vermouth and gin; an Americano, a mix of Campari, red vermouth and soda; or a spritz, made from Aperol or Campari and *prosecco* sparkling wine.

The Buffet

Where in the past you might have been served a bowl of olives and salty nuts, now bars go all out to impress with their lavish buffet displays. These vary from place to place, and some bars have their own specialities, but a typical spread might include olive-stuffed pastries, bite-sized frittatas, pasta salads, mini-pizzas, bowls of spicy couscous, steaming risottos, grilled vegetables, cheeses and cold cuts. Play your cards right and you might well find you've had dinner for little more than the price of a drink. But while it may be tempting to pile that plate sky high, don't forget that this is the land of *la bella figura*, where looking cool is good, and canapé landslides are not. Do like the locals do and stuff yourself *discreetly*.

Top Spots

For a classy fill-up, don't miss the evening spread at hit Trastevere haunt Freni e Frizioni (p121) or the rich banquet laid on by the fashionable Ostiense bar Doppiozeroo (p107). The historic Pigneto hang-out Necci (p79) offers a relaxed bohemian atmosphere, while Etablì (p50) is a hip hang-out in the historic centre.

Explore

Vatican City
& Prati

The Vatican, the world's smallest sovereign state (0.44 sq km), sits over the river from the *centro storico* (historic centre). Centred on the domed St Peter's Basilica, it's a spiritual, artistic and touristic super-power, home to some of the world's most famous works of art and hundreds of overpriced restaurants and souvenir shops. It's busy by day but at night the action shifts to the restaurants in nearby Prati.

The Sights in a Day

Beat the queues and get to the **Vatican Museums** (p132) at the crack of dawn. These museums house one of the world's great art collections, and while you'll never manage to see everything in one visit, you'll want to check out the **Cortile Ottagono** (p133), home to some amazing classical sculpture, the vibrantly frescoed **Stanze di Raffaello** (Raphael Rooms) (p134), and, of course, the **Sistine Chapel** (p134). Afterwards, reflect on what you've seen over a light lunch at **Il Sorpasso** (p144).

After lunch, head to **St Peter's Square** (p142), the dramatic gateway to **St Peter's Basilica** (p136), the Vatican's imperious showcase church. Explore the awe-inspiring marble-clad interior and climb the dome before heading down Via della Conciliazione to round off the afternoon at the landmark **Castel Sant'Angelo** (p142).

Come evening, treat yourself to some high-quality cuisine at **Romeo** (p143) before retiring to jazz mecca **Alexanderplatz** (p145) to see out the day with a concert.

Top Sights

Vatican Museums (p132)

St Peter's Basilica (p136)

Best of Rome

Architecture
St Peter's Basilica (p136)

St Peter's Square (p142)

Art & Museums
Vatican Museums (p132)

Sistine Chapel (p134)

Pietà, St Peter's Basilica (p136)

La scuola di Atene (The School of Athens) (p134)

Castel Sant'Angelo (p142)

Eating
Pizzarium (p142)

Ristorante L'Arcangelo (p143)

Getting There

M Metro Take metro line A to Ottaviano–San Pietro.

🚌 Bus From Termini, bus 40 is the quickest option – it'll drop you off near Castel Sant'Angelo. Bus 64 covers a similar route but stops more often. Bus 492 runs to Piazza del Risorgimento from Stazione Tiburtina, passing through Piazza Barberini and the *centro storico* (historic centre).

Top Sights
Vatican Museums

Visiting the Vatican Museums is a thrilling and unforgettable experience. With some 7km of exhibitions and more masterpieces than many small countries, this vast museum complex contains one of the world's greatest art collections. Highlights include a spectacular collection of classical statuary, a suite of rooms painted by Raphael, and the Michelangelo-decorated Sistine Chapel. Housing it all is the 5.5-hectare Palazzo Apostolico Vaticano, which also serves as the pope's official residence.

Map p140, C3

06 6988 4676

http://mv.vatican.va

Viale Vaticano

adult/reduced €16/8, last Sunday of month free

9am-4pm Mon-Sat, 9am-12.30pm last Sun of month

Ottaviano-San Pietro

Spiral staircase at the Vatican Museums

Don't Miss

Pinacoteca

Often overlooked by visitors, the papal gallery contains Raphael's last work, *La Trasfigurazione* (Transfiguration; 1517–20), and paintings by Giotto, Fra Angelico, Filippo Lippi, Perugino, Titian, Guido Reni, Guercino, Pietro da Cortona, Caravaggio and Leonardo da Vinci, whose haunting *San Gerolamo* (St Jerome; c 1480) was never finished.

Cortile della Pigna

One of three internal courtyards, the Cortile della Pigna takes its name from the huge Augustan-era bronze pine cone that sits in the courtyard's great niche. In the centre, the 4m-diameter ball, the *Sfera,* is by Italian sculptor Arnaldo Pomodoro.

Museo Pio-Clementino – Cortile Ottagono

This octagonal courtyard contains some of the Vatican Museums' finest classical statuary, including the peerless *Apollo Belvedere,* a Roman copy of a 4th-century-BC Greek bronze depicting the sun god Apollo, and the 1st-century *Laocoön,* representing a muscular Trojan priest and his two sons in mortal struggle against two sea serpents.

Museo Pio-Clementino – Inside Rooms

Beyond the Cortile Ottagono, the **Sala delle Muse** is centred on the *Torso Belvedere,* a 1st-century-BC Greek sculpture that was used by Michelangelo as a model for his *ignudi* (nude figures) in the Sistine Chapel. The **Sala Rotonda** features an enormous red basin found at Nero's Domus Aurea.

Chiaramonti, Etruscan & Egyptian Museums

Other notable museums include the **Museo Chiaramonti**, where thousands of statues line the long corridor that runs down the lower east flank

☑ Top Tips

▶ The museums are free on the last Sunday of the month.

▶ To avoid queues, book tickets and guided tours online at http://biglietteriamusei.vatican.va/musei/tickets/do (plus €4 booking fee).

▶ Time your visit to minimise waiting: Wednesday mornings are good; afternoon is better than the morning; avoid Mondays when many other museums are shut.

▶ The *Guide to the Vatican Museums and City* (€14) is a sound investment, as exhibits are not well labelled.

✗ Take a Break

There's a self-service restaurant and bar near the Pinacoteca, and another bar on the stairs to the Sistine Chapel. But for a real taste to remember, leave the museums and head to Pizzarium (p142), one of Rome's best *pizza al taglio* (pizza by the slice) joints.

of the Belvedere Palace; the **Museo Gregoriano Etrusco**, home to the 4th-century-BC *Marte di Todi* (Mars of Todi) and innumerable Etruscan aretfacts; and the **Museo Gregoriano Egizio**, which displays pieces taken from Egypt in Roman times.

Galleria delle Carte Geografiche

One of the unsung heroes of the Vatican Museums, the 120m-long Map Gallery is hung with 40 huge topographical maps. These were all created between 1580 and 1583 for Pope Gregory XIII, and based on drafts by Ignazio Danti, one of the leading cartographers of the day.

Stanze di Raffaello (Raphael Rooms)

These four frescoed rooms comprised Pope Julius II's private apartment. But while they carry Raphael's name, he only actually painted two – the **Stanza della Segnatura** (Study; 1508–11) and the **Stanza di Eliodoro** (Waiting Room; 1512–14). The **Stanza dell'Incendio** (Dining Room; 1514–17) and the **Sala di Costantino** (Reception Room; 1517–24) were decorated by students working to his designs.

Stanze di Raffaello – La Scuola di Atene

Of the frescoes in the Raphael Rooms, the greatest is *The School of Athens* in the Stanza della Segnatura. Depicting scholars gathered around Plato and Aristotle, it includes some notable portraits – the figure in front of the steps is believed to be Michelangelo;

Plato's face is supposedly that of Leonardo da Vinci; and the second figure from the right is Raphael himself.

Sistine Chapel

Named after Pope Sixtus IV, the 15th-century Sistine Chapel (Cappella Sistina) is home to two of the world's most famous works of art – Michelangelo's ceiling frescoes and his *Giudizio universale* – as well as a series of superlative wall frescoes. It also serves an important religious function as the chapel where the conclave meets to elect a new pope.

Sistine Chapel – Ceiling Frescoes

Painted between 1508 and 1512, the 800-sq-metre ceiling design represents nine scenes from the book of Genesis. The most famous is the *Creation of Adam,* which shows God pointing his figure at Adam, thus bringing him to life. Framing the scenes are painted architectural features and 20 muscular *ignudi* (athletic male nudes).

Sistine Chapel – Giudizio Universale

Covering the 200-sq-metre west wall, Michelangelo's highly charged *Giudizio universale* (Last Judgment; 1535–41) depicts the souls of the dead being torn from their graves to face God's judgment. When it was unveiled, its swirling mass of naked bodies caused controversy – Pope Pius IV later had Daniele da Volterra add fig leaves and loincloths to 41 nudes.

Vatican Museums

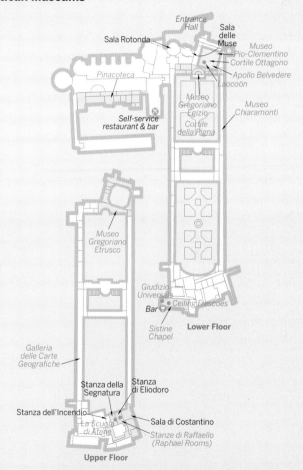

Entrance Hall

Sala Rotonda

Sala delle Muse

Museo Pio-Clementino

Cortile Ottagono

Apollo Belvedere

Laocoön

Pinacoteca

Museo Chiaramonti

Self-service restaurant & bar

Museo Gregoriano Egizio

Cortile della Pigna

Museo Gregoriano Etrusco

Giudizio Universale

Bar — Ceiling Frescoes

Lower Floor

Sistine Chapel

Galleria delle Carte Geografiche

Stanza della Segnatura

Stanza di Eliodoro

Stanza dell'Incendio

Sala di Costantino

La Scuola di Atene

Stanze di Raffaello (Raphael Rooms)

Upper Floor

Top Sights
St Peter's Basilica

Few churches can hold a candle to St Peter's Basilica (Basilica di San Pietro), one of the world's largest, richest and most spectacular cathedrals. The current church, the world's second largest (after the Basilica of Our Lady of Peace in Yamoussoukro, Ivory Coast), was built over the original 4th-century basilica and completed in 1626 after 150 years' construction. It contains some brilliant works of art, including three celebrated masterpieces: Michelangelo's *Pietà*, his breathtaking dome, and Bernini's baldachin (canopy) over the papal altar.

◉ Map p140, C4

www.vatican.va

St Peter's Sq

admission free

⌚ 7am-7pm summer, to 6.30pm winter

Ⓜ Ottaviano-San Pietro

Bernini's baldachin in the centre of the basilica

Don't Miss

The Facade

Completed in 1612, Carlo Maderno's immense facade features eight 27m-high columns and 13 statues representing Christ, St John the Baptist, and the 11 apostles. The central balcony, the **Loggia della Benedizione,** is where the pope stands to deliver his Christmas and Easter blessing.

In the grand atrium, the **Porta Santa** (Holy Door) is opened only in Jubilee Years.

Pietà

At the beginning of the right aisle, Michelangelo's hauntingly beautiful *Pietà* sits in its own chapel behind a panel of bullet-proof glass. Sculpted when the artist was a little-known 25-year-old (in 1499), it's the only work he ever signed – his signature is etched into the sash across the Madonna's breast.

Cappella del Santissimo Sacramento

Next to the **Cappella di San Sebastiano**, home of Pope John Paul II's tomb, the Cappella del Santissimo Sacramento is a small, sumptuously decorated baroque chapel. The iron grille was designed by Borromini, the gilt bronze ciborium over the altar is by Bernini, and the altarpiece is by Pietro da Cortona.

Baldachin

Dominating the centre of the basilica is Bernini's 29m-high baldachin. Supported by four spiral columns and made with bronze taken from the Pantheon, it stands over the **papal altar**, also known as the Altar of the Confession. In front, Carlo Maderno's **Confessione** stands over the site where St Peter was originally buried.

☑ Top Tips

▸ Dress appropriately if you want to get in – no shorts, miniskirts or bare shoulders.

▸ Free English-language tours of the basilica are run from the Centro Servizi Pellegrini e Turisti at 9am every Tuesday and Thursday.

▸ Queues are inevitable at the security checks, but they move quickly.

▸ Lines are generally shorter during lunch hours and late afternoon.

▸ Be aware that pick-pockets operate in the Vatican, so keep watch of your valuables.

✗ Take a Break

Avoid the tourist traps around the basilica and head to nearby Prati. For a sinful snack, stop off at the Sicilian gelateria Gelarmony (p144), while for something more substantial, enjoy a traditional Roman lunch at Velavevodetto Ai Quiriti (p143).

Dome

Above the baldachin, Michelangelo's dome soars to a height of 119m. Based on Brunelleschi's cupola in Florence, it's supported by four stone piers named after the saints whose statues adorn their Bernini-designed niches – Longinus, Helena, Veronica and Andrew. To climb the **dome** (with/ without lift €7/5; ☉8am-5.45pm summer, to 4.45pm winter), head to the entrance to the right of the basilica.

Statue of St Peter

At the base of the Pier of St Longinus is a much-loved bronze statue of St Peter, whose right foot has been worn down by centuries of caresses. It is believed to be a 13th-century work by

Arnolfo di Cambio. On the Feast Day of St Peter and St Paul (29 June), the statue is dressed in papal robes.

Cattedra di San Pietro

Dominating the tribune behind the papal altar is Bernini's extraordinary Cattedra di San Pietro (Chair of St Peter). A vast gilded bronze throne held aloft by four 5m-high saints, it's centred on a wooden seat that was once thought to have been St Peter's but in fact dates to the 9th century.

Monument to Alexander VII

To the left of the baldachin is one of the basilica's most dramatic works, the monument to Alexander VII. Featuring a billowing marble drape

St Peter's Basilica

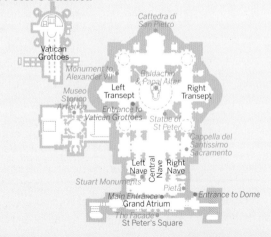

Understand
Christina, Queen of Sweden

On a pillar just beyond Michelangelo's *Pietà* is Carlo Fontana's **monument to Queen Christina of Sweden**, a woman whose reputation was far from holy. Famously portrayed by Greta Garbo in the 1933 film *Queen Christina,* the Swedish monarch is one of only three women buried in the basilica – the other two are Queen Charlotte of Cyprus, a minor 15th-century royal, and Agnesina Colonna, a 16th-century Italian aristocrat. Christina earned her place by abdicating the Swedish throne and converting to Catholicism in 1655. As Europe's most high-profile convert, she became a Vatican favourite and spent much of her later life in Rome, where she enjoyed fame as a brilliant patron of the arts. Her active private life was the subject of much salacious gossip and rumours abounded of affairs with courtiers and acquaintances of both sexes.

held aloft by a creepy bronze skeleton with an hourglass in its hand, this was Bernini's last work in the basilica, completed in 1678.

Stuart Monuments

One of the few monuments in the basilica not commemorating a pope, Antonio Canova's vaguely erotic white marble tablet is dedicated to the last three members of the Stuart clan – James Francis Edward Stuart and his two sons, Bonnie Prince Charlie and Henry – the pretenders to the English throne who died in exile in Rome.

Museo Storico Artistico

The **Museo Storico Artistico** (Tesoro; adult/reduced €7/5; ☉9am-6.15pm summer, to 5.15pm winter) showcases the basilica's sacred relics and priceless artefacts. Highlights include a tabernacle by Donatello; the Colonna Santa, a 4th-

century Byzantine column from the earlier church; and the 6th-century *Crux vaticana* (Vatican Cross), a gift from the emperor Justinian II.

Vatican Grottoes

Extending beneath the basilica, the **Vatican Grottoes** (admission free; ☉9am-6pm summer, to 5pm winter) contain the tombs of numerous popes, as well as columns from the original 4th-century basilica. The entrance is in the Pier of St Andrew.

Tomb of St Peter

Excavations beneath the basilica have uncovered part of the original church and what archaeologists believe is the **Tomb of St Peter** (☎06 6988 5318; admission €13, over 15s only). The excavations can only be visited by guided tour. To book a spot, email the **Ufficio Scavi** (scavi@fsp.va) as early as possible.

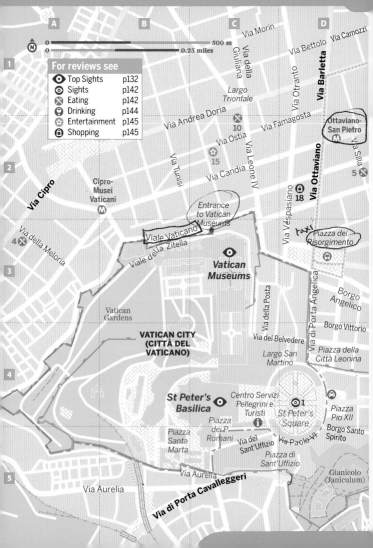

N

0   500 m
0   0.25 miles

For reviews see

◉	Top Sights	p132
◉	Sights	p142
✗	Eating	p142
🍷	Drinking	p144
★	Entertainment	p145
🛍	Shopping	p145

Via Morin

Via della Giuliana

Via Bettolo

Via Camozzi

Largo Trionfale

Via Otranto

Via Barletta

Via Andrea Doria

✗ 10

Via Famagosta

Ottaviano-San Pietro Ⓜ

Via Ostia

Via Silla

Via Candia

Via Leone IV

5 ✗

Via Tunisi

Via Ottaviano

Via Cipro

Cipro-Musei Vaticani Ⓜ

Via Véspasiano

🛍 18

Via della Meloria

Entrance to Vatican Museums

Viale Vaticano

Via di Porta Angelica

Piazza del Risorgimento

4 ✗

Viale della Zitella

Vatican Museums ◉

Borgo Angelico

Via della Posta

Borgo Vittorio

Vatican Gardens

VATICAN CITY (CITTÀ DEL VATICANO)

Via del Belvedere

Piazza della Città Leonina

Largo San Martino

St Peter's Basilica ◉

Centro Servizi Pellegrini e Turisti ℹ

St Peter's Square ◉ 1

Piazza Pio XII

Piazza Santa Marta

Piazza dei P Romani

Borgo Santo Spirito

Via del Sant'Uffizio

Via Paolo VI

Piazza di Sant'Uffizio

Via Aurelia

Gianicolo (Janiculum)

Via Aurelia

Via di Porta Cavalleggeri

Viale delle Milizie

Via C A Dalla Chiesa

PRATI

Via Caio Mario

11

Via Germanico

Via delle Milizie

Via Damiata

Viale Giulio Cesare

Via Duilio

Via Fabio Massimo

Via Emilio

Lepanto M

Via degli Scipioni

Via Ezio

Piazza dei Quiriti

6

Via Lepanto

Via Farnese

Via Vigliena

Via Vigliena

Via Marcantonio Colonna

8

Via Pompeo Magno

Via dei Gracchi

Ponte P Nenni

Piazza della Libertà

Ponte Margherita

12

Via Cola di Rienzo

Via dei Gracchi

Via Valadier

Via Ennio Quirini Visconti

Lgt dei Mellini

Varrone

16

Via Properzio

Via Tibullo

Via Terenzio

Via Catullo

Via Della Valle

Via Boezio

Via Cassiodoro

Via Plinio

Via Orazio

Via Tacito

Via Cicerone

7

Via Lucrezio Caro

Via Gioachino Belli

Via Pietro Cossa

Via Marianna Dionigi

13

9

Via S Porcari

Via Cancelleri

Via Crescenzio

Via Alberico II

Largo di Porta Castello

Piazza Adriana

Giardini di Castel Sant'Angelo

17

Piazza Cavour

Via Tribuniano

Via Ulpiano

Lgt Prati

Borgo Pio

Borgo Sant'Angelo

Piazza Pia

Castel Sant'Angelo

2

Lgt Castello

Ponte Umberto I

Lgt Marzio

Via della Conciliazione

Largo I Gregore

Via di Porta Santo Spirito

Lgt in Sassia

Via San Pio

Ponte Principe Amedeo

Lgt della Fiorentini

Ponte Vittorio Emanuele II

Piazza dell'Oro

3 Ponte Sant'Angelo

Corso Vittorio Emanuele II

Tiber River

Piazza di San Salvatore in Lauro

Piazza Lacellotti

Via dei Coronari

Piazza di Monte Vecchio

Lgt Tor di Nona

Ponte Umberto I

Via dell'Orso

Piazza Febo

Largo Febo

Beautiful street of shops

Sights

St Peter's Square

PIAZZA

1 Map p140, D4

Overlooked by St Peter's Basilica, the Vatican's central square was laid out between 1656 and 1667 to a design by Gian Lorenzo Bernini. Seen from above, it resembles a giant keyhole with two semicircular colonnades, each consisting of four rows of Doric columns, encircling a giant ellipse that straightens out to funnel believers into the basilica. The effect was deliberate – Bernini described the colonnades as representing 'the motherly arms of the church'. (Piazza San Pietro; M Ottaviano-San Pietro)

Castel Sant'Angelo

MUSEUM, CASTLE

2 Map p140, F4

With its chunky round keep, this castle is an instantly recognisable landmark. Built as a mausoleum for the emperor Hadrian, it was converted into a papal fortress in the 6th century and named after an angelic vision that Pope Gregory the Great had in 590. Nowadays, it houses the **Museo Nazionale di Castel Sant'Angelo** and its eclectic collection of paintings, sculpture, military memorabilia and medieval firearms. (✆ 06 681 91 11; http://castelsantangelo.beni-culturali.it; Lungotevere Castello 50; adult/reduced €7/3.50; ⊙ 9am-7.30pm Tue-Sun; 🚌 Piazza Pia)

Ponte Sant'Angelo

BRIDGE

3 Map p140, F4

The emperor Hadrian built the Ponte Sant'Angelo in AD 136 to provide an approach to his mausoleum, but it was Bernini who brought it to life, designing the angel sculptures in 1668. The three central arches of the bridge are part of the original structure; the end arches were enlarged in 1892–94 during the construction of the Lungotevere embankments. (🚌 Piazza Pia)

Eating

Pizzarium

PIZZA €

4 Map p140, A3

Pizzarium, or 'Bonci pizza rustica #pizzarium', as it has recently rebranded itself, serves some of Rome's best sliced pizza. Scissor-cut squares of meticulously crafted dough are topped with original combinations of seasonal ingredients and served on paper trays

---

☑ Top Tip

Meet the Pope

At 11am each Wednesday, the pope addresses his flock at the Vatican (in July and August in Castel Gandolfo near Rome). For details on free tickets, see www.vatican.va/various/prefettura/index_en.html.

When he's in Vatican City, the Pope blesses the crowd in St Peter's Square on Sunday at noon. No tickets are required.

for immediate consumption. There's also a daily selection of freshly fried *supplì* (crunchy rice croquettes). (Via della Meloria 43; pizza slices from €3; ⏰11am-10pm; 🚇Cipro-Musei Vaticani)

Romeo
PIZZA, RISTORANTE €€

5 🍴 Map p140, D2

This chic, contemporary outfit is part bakery, part deli, part takeaway, and part restaurant. For a quick bite, there's delicious sliced pizza or you can have a *panino* (sandwich) made up at the deli counter; for a full restaurant meal, the à la carte menu offers a mix of traditional Italian dishes and forward-looking international creations. (📞06 3211 0120; www.romeo.roma.it; Via Silla 26a; pizza slices €2.50, meals €45; ⏰9am-midnight; 🚇Ottaviano-San Pietro)

Velavevodetto Ai Quiriti
LAZIO CUISINE €€

6 🍴 Map p140, F2

This welcoming restaurant continues to win diners over with its unpretentious, earthy food and honest prices. The menu reads like a directory of Roman staples, and while it's all pretty good, standout choices include *fettuccine con asparagi, guanciale e pecorino* (pasta ribbons with asparagus, guanciale and pecorino cheese) and *polpette di bollito* (fried meat balls). (📞06 3600 0009; www.ristorantevelavevodetto.it; Piazza dei Quiriti 5; meals €35; ⏰12.30-2.30pm & 7.30-11.30pm; 🚇Lepanto)

Ponte Sant'Angelo

Ristorante L'Arcangelo
RISTORANTE €€€

7 🍴 Map p140, G3

Styled as an informal bistro with wood-panelling, leather banquettes and casual table settings, L'Arcangelo enjoys a stellar local reputation. The highlight for many are the classic Roman staples such as carbonara and *amatriciana* (pasta with spicy tomato sauce), but there's also a limited selection of more innovative modern dishes. The wine list is a further plus, boasting some interesting Italian labels. (📞06 321 09 92; www.larcangelo.com; Via Belli 59-61; tasting menus lunch/dinner €25/55, meals €60; ⏰12.30-2.30pm Mon-Fri, 8-11pm Mon-Sat; 🚌Piazza Cavour)

Gelarmony
GELATERIA €

8 Map p140, G2

Sweet-tooths are spoiled for choice at this popular Sicilian gelateria. There's an ample selection of fruit and cream gelati but for a typically Sicilian flavour go for pistachio or cassata. (Via Marcantonio Colonna 34; gelato €1.50-3; ⏱10am-late; Ⓜ Lepanto)

Il Sorpasso
ITALIAN €€

9 Map p140, E3

A bar-restaurant hybrid sporting a vintage cool look – vaulted stone ceilings, hanging hams, white bare-brick walls – Il Sorpasso is a hot ticket right now. Open throughout the day, it caters to a fashionable neighbourhood crowd, serving everything from pasta specials to *aperitivo* (bar buffet), *trappizini* (pyramids of stuffed pizza), and a full dinner menu. (www.sorpasso.info; meals €20-35; ⏱7am-1am Mon-Fri, 9am-1am Sat; 🚇Piazza del Risorgimento)

Hostaria Dino e Tony
TRATTORIA €€

10 Map p140, C2

An authentic old-school trattoria, Dino e Tony offers simple, no-frills Roman cooking. Kick off with the monumental antipasto, a minor meal in its own right, before plunging into the trattoria's signature *rigatoni all'amatriciana* (pasta tubes with baconlike *guanciale*, chilli and tomato sauce). No credit cards. (📞06 3973 3284; Via Leone IV 60; meals €25-30; ⏱12.30-3pm & 7-11pm, closed Sun & Aug; Ⓜ Ottaviano-San Pietro)

Del Frate
RISTORANTE, WINE BAR €€

11 Map p140, E2

Locals love this upmarket wine bar with its simple wooden tables and high-ceilinged rooms. There's a formidable wine and cheese list with everything from Sicilian ricotta to Piedmontese gorgonzola, and a small, refined menu. (📞06 323 64 37; www.enotecadelfrate.it; Via degli Scipioni 122; meals €40; ⏱noon-3pm & 6pm-11.45 Mon-Sat; Ⓜ Ottaviano-San Pietro)

Drinking

Sciascia Caffè
CAFE

12 Map p140, E2

The timeless elegance of this polished cafe is perfectly suited to the exquisite coffee it makes. There are various options but nothing can beat the *caffè eccellente,* a velvety smooth espresso served in a delicate cup that has been lined with melted chocolate. (Via Fabio Massimo 80/A; ⏱7.30am-6.30pm Mon-Sat; Ⓜ Ottaviano-San Pietro)

Passaguai
WINE BAR

13 Map p140, E3

A cosy basement bar on a quiet side-street, Passaguai feels pleasingly off-the-radar. It's a great spot for a beer or glass of wine – there's an excellent choice of both – accompanied by cheese and cold cuts, or even a full meal from the limited menu. Free wi-fi. (📞06 8745 1358; www.passaguai.it; Via Leto 1; ⏱10am-2am Mon-Fri, 6pm-2am Sat & Sun; 🛜; 🚇Piazza del Risorgimento)

Makasar
WINE BAR, TEAHOUSE

14 Map p140, E3

Recharge your batteries with a quiet drink at this oasis of bookish tranquility. Pick your tipple from the nine-page tea menu or opt for an Italian wine and sit back. For something to eat, there's a small menu of salads, bruschette, baguettes and healthy hot dishes. (www.makasar.it; Via Plauto 33; ☉noon-midnight Tue-Thu, to 2am Fri & Sat, 5.30-11.30pm Sun; ☐Piazza del Risorgimento)

Entertainment

Alexanderplatz
JAZZ

15 Map p140, C2

Small, intimate and underground, Rome's most celebrated jazz club draws top Italian and international performers and a respectful cosmopolitan crowd. Book a table for the best stage views or if you want to dine to the tunes. Check the website for upcoming gigs. (☑06 3972 1867; www.alexanderplatzjazzclub.com; Via Ostia 9; ☉8.30pm-2am, concerts 9.45pm; Ⓜ Ottaviano-San Pietro)

Fonclea
LIVE MUSIC

16 Map p140, E3

Fonclea is a great little pub venue, serving up nightly gigs by bands playing everything from jazz and soul to funk, rock and Latin (concerts start at around 9.30pm). Get in the mood with a drink during happy hour (7pm to 8.30pm daily). From June to August, the pub ups sticks and moves to a site by the Tiber. (☑06 689 63 02; www.fonclea.it; Via Crescenzio 82a; ☉7pm-2am Sep-May; ☐Piazza del Risorgimento)

Shopping

Enoteca Costantini
WINE

17 Map p140, G3

If you're after a hard-to-find grappa or something special for your wine collection, this historic *enoteca* (wine bar) is the place to try. Opened in 1972, Piero Costantini's superbly stocked shop is a point of reference for aficionados across town with its 800-sq-metre basement cellar and a colossal collection of wines and spirits. (www.piero costantini.it; Piazza Cavour 16; ☉9am-1pm Tue-Sat, 4.30-8pm Mon-Sat; ☐Piazza Cavour)

Antica Manufattura Cappelli
ACCESSORIES

18 Map p140, D2

A throwback to a more elegant age, the atelier-boutique of milliner Patrizia Fabri offers a wide range of beautifully crafted hats. Choose from the off-the-peg line of straw Panamas, vintage cloches, felt berets and tweed deerstalkers, or have one made to measure. Prices range from about €70 to €300 and ordered hats can be delivered within the day. (☑06 3972 5679; www.antica-cappelleria.it; Via degli Scipioni 46; ☉9am-7pm Mon-Fri; Ⓜ Ottaviano-San Pietro)

Top Sights
Villa Borghese

Getting There

M **Metro** The best options are Spagna (line A) or Flaminio (line A).

🚌 **Bus** Take bus 116 or 53 from Via Vittorio Veneto.

Villa Borghese, Rome's best-known park, is a lush, landscaped oasis of green. The ideal spot to recharge your batteries, it was once the estate of a powerful 17th-century cardinal and today covers about 80 hectares of wooded glades, gardens and grassy banks. Among its myriad attractions are several excellent museums, including the peerless Museo e Galleria Borghese, the landscaped Giardino del Lago, and Piazza di Siena, a dusty arena used for Rome's top equestrian event in May.

19th-century temple, Giardino del Lago, Villa Borghese

Don't Miss

Museo e Galleria Borghese

One of Rome's best museums, the **Museo e Galleria Borghese** (📞06 3 28 10; www.galleriaborghese.it; Piazzale del Museo Borghese 5; adult/reduced €11/6.50; ⊙9am-7pm Tue-Sun; 🚇Via Pinciana) harbours what's often referred to as the 'queen of all private art collections'. This spectacular treasure trove of Renaissance and baroque art, amassed by Cardinal Scipione Borghese and housed in his lavishly decorated 17th-century villa, includes paintings by Caravaggio, Raphael and Titian, and a series of sensational mythical sculptures by Gian Lorenzo Bernini. Masterpieces abound, but look out for Bernini's *Ratto di Proserpina* (Rape of Proserpina) and Canova's *Venere Vincitrice* (Venus Victrix).

To limit numbers, visitors are admitted at two-hourly intervals, so you'll need to prebook your ticket and get an entry time.

Museo Nazionale Etrusco di Villa Giulia

Pope Julius III's 16th-century villa provides the charming setting for the **Museo Nazionale Etrusco di Villa Giulia** (www.villagiulia.beniculturali.it; Piazzale di Villa Giulia; adult/reduced €8/4; ⊙8.30am-7.30pm Tue-Sun; 🚇Via delle Belle Arti), home to Italy's finest collection of Etruscan treasures. Among its prized exhibits are the 6th-century-BC *Sarcofago degli Sposi* (Sarcophagus of the Betrothed); a polychrome terracotta statue of *Apollo;* and the *Euphronios Krater,* a celebrated Greek vase.

---

entrances at Piazzale San Paolo del Brasile, Piazzale Flaminio, Via Pinciana, Via Raimondo, Largo Pablo Picasso

---

⊙dawn-dusk

🚇Porta Pinciana

☑ Top Tips

▶ Villa Borghese's museums and galleries are open Tuesday to Sunday.

▶ Remember to prebook your ticket for the Museo e Galleria Borghese.

✕ Take a Break

For a refined break, search out the **Caffè delle Arti** (📞06 3265 1236; www.caffedellearti roma.com; Via Gramsci 73; meal €45; ⊙12.30-3.30pm daily & 7.30-11pm Tue-Sun; 🚇Piazza Thorvaldsen), the elegant cafe-cum-restaurant of the Galleria Nazionale d'Arte Moderna e Contemporanea (p148). It's at its best on sultry summer evenings when you can sit on the terrace and enjoy coffees, cocktails or a full à la carte dinner.

Galleria Nazionale d'Arte Moderna e Contemporanea

Housed in a vast belle époque palace, the **Galleria Nazionale d'Arte Moderna e Contemporanea** (☏06 3229 8221; www. gnam.beniculturali.it; Viale delle Belle Arti 131, disabled entrance Via Gramsci 73; adult/reduced €8/4; ⏱8.30am-7.30pm Tue-Sun; 🚊Piazza Thorvaldsen) is an unsung gem of a museum. Its superlative collection includes works by a roll-call of important 19th- and 20th-century artists, including Canova, Modigliani, Van Gogh, Monet, Klimt, Giacometti and Henry Moore.

Museo Carlo Bilotti

Charmingly ensconced in the Orangery of Villa Borghese, the **Museo Carlo Bilotti** (☏06 06 08; www.museo carlobilotti.it; Viale Fiorello La Guardia; admission free; ⏱10am-4pm Tue-Fri winter, 1-7pm Tue-Fri summer, 10am-7pm Sat & Sun year-round; 🚊Porta Pinciana) houses the art collection of billionaire Carlo Bilotti. The main focus are 18 works by Giorgio de Chirico (1888–1978) but also of note is a Warhol portrait of Bilotti's wife and daughter.

Nearby: Auditorium Parco della Musica

To the north of Villa Borghese, the Renzo Piano–designed **Auditorium Parco della Musica** (☏06 8024 1281; www.auditorium.com; Viale Pietro de Coubertin 30; 🚊Viale Tiziano) is Rome's flagship cultural centre and concert venue. Its three concert halls offer superb acoustics, and, together with a 3000-seat open-air arena, stage everything from classical-music concerts to jazz gigs, public lectures, and film screenings.

Nearby: Museo Nazionale delle Arti del XXI Secolo (MAXXI)

Rome's flagship contemporary art museum is the **Museo Nazionale delle Arti del XXI Secolo** (☏06 320 19 54; www.fondazionemaxxi.it; Via Guido Reni 4a; adult/reduced €11/8; ⏱11am-7pm Tue-Fri & Sun, to 10pm Sat; 🚊Viale Tiziano), aka MAXXI. Housed in a Zaha Hadid–converted former barracks, it has a small permanent collection and hosts temporary exhibitions and installations.

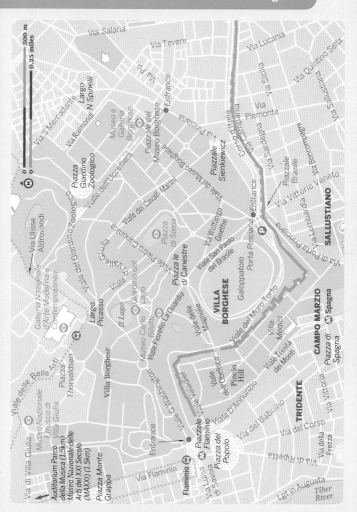

500 m
0.25 miles

Via Salaria

Via Tevere

Via Lucania

Via Quintino Sella

Via S Mercadante

Via Raimondi N Spinelli

Largo
Raimondi N Spinelli

Via Po

Entrance

Piazzale del
Museo Borghese

Via Sicilia

Via Piemonte

Corso d'Italia

Via Sallustiana

Museo e
Galleria
Borghese

Piazza
Giardino
Zoologico

Viale dell'Uccelliera

Viale del Museo Borghese

Via Pinciana

Piazza
Sienkiewicz

Via Campania

Via Sardegna

Piazzale
Brasile

Via Vittorio Veneto

SALLUSTIANO

Via di Porta Pinciana

Via Ulisse
Aldrovandi

Viale del Giardino Zoologico

Viale dei Cavalli Marini

Piazza
di Siena

Via Wolfango
Goethe

Viale San Paolo
del Brasile

Porta Pinciana

Via di Porta Pinciana

Via di Porta Lombarda

Galleria Nazionale
d'Arte Moderna e
Contemporanea

Via Giulia

Giardino del
Lago

Piazzale
di Canestre

Galoppatoio

VILLA
BORGHESE

Viale Pietro Canonica

Largo
Picasso

Il Lago

Museo Carlo
Bilotti

Viale Fiorello La Guardia

Viale delle
Magnolie

Viale del Muro Torto

Villa
Medici

CAMPO MARZIO

Spagna

Viale delle Belle Arti

Piazza
Thorvaldsen

Villa Borghese

Viale Washington

Viale Goethe

Viale dell'Obelisco

Pincio
Hill

Viale Trinità
dei Monti

Piazza di
Spagna

Museo Nazionale
Etrusco di
Villa Giulia

Via di Villa Giulia

Auditorium Parco
della Musica (1.5km)
Museo Nazionale delle
Arti del XXI Secolo
(MAXXI) (1.5km)
Piazza Monte
Grappa

Entrance

Viale G Washington

Viale Valadier

Piazzale
Flaminio

Viale D'Annunzio

Via del Babuino

TRIDENTE

Via Vittoria

Via della
Freza

Via del Corso

Flaminio

Via Luisa
di Savoia

Piazza del
Popolo

Via Flaminia

Via di Ripetta

Lgt in Augusta

Tiber
River

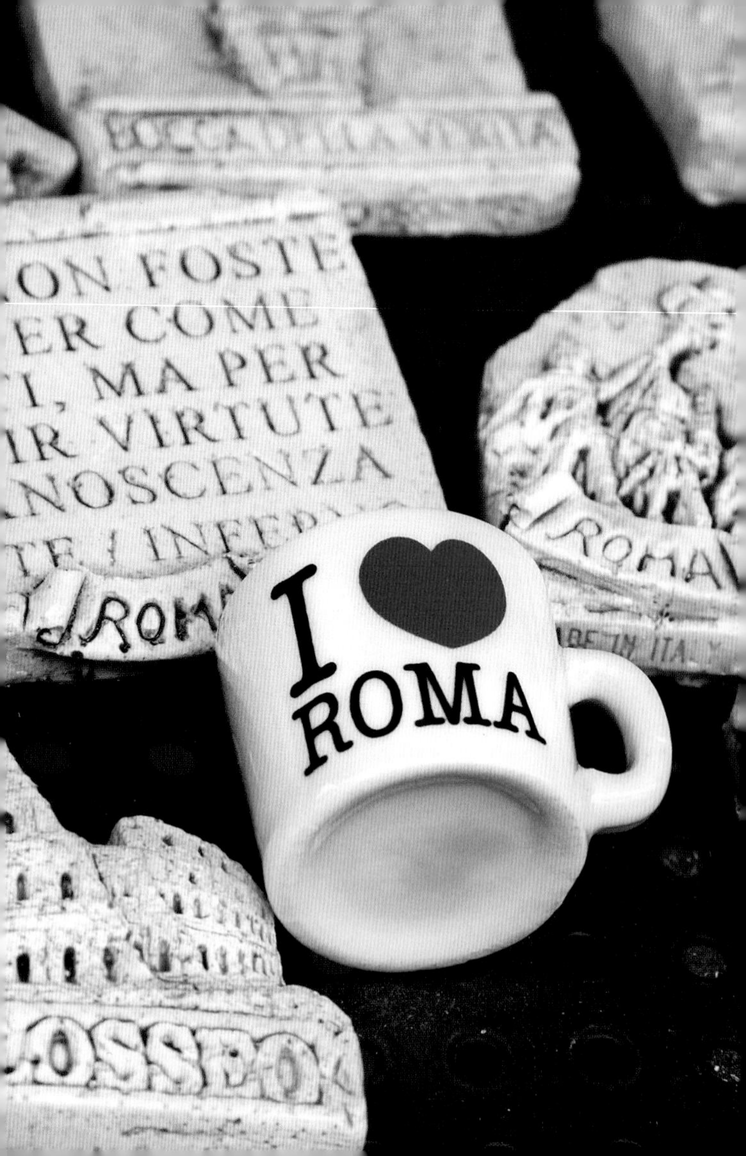
ON FOSTE
ER COME
I, MA PER
IR VIRTUTE
NOSCENZA
ROMA
I
ROMA
ROMA

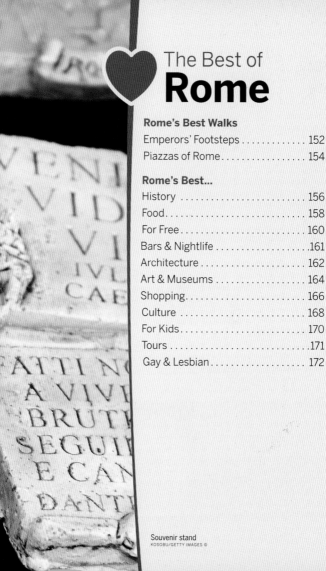

The Best of
Rome

Rome's Best Walks

Emperors' Footsteps 152
Piazzas of Rome 154

Rome's Best...

History 156
Food 158
For Free 160
Bars & Nightlife 161
Architecture 162
Art & Museums 164
Shopping 166
Culture 168
For Kids 170
Tours 171
Gay & Lesbian 172

Souvenir stand
KOSOBU/GETTY IMAGES ©

Best Walks
Emperors' Footsteps

🏃 The Walk

Follow in the footsteps of Rome's legendary emperors on this walk around the best of the city's ancient treasures. Established in 27 BC, the Roman Empire grew to become the Western world's first dominant superpower and at the peak of its power, in about AD 100, it extended from Britain to north Africa, and from Syria to Spain. Rome had a population of more than 1.5 million and all of the trappings of imperial splendour: marble temples, public baths, theatres, shopping centres and, of course, the Colosseum.

Start Colosseum; Ⓜ Colosseo

Finish Il Vittoriano; 🚊 Piazza Venezia

Length 1.5km; at least three hours

🍴 Take a Break

Hidden away in the Capitoline Museums but accessible by its own entrance, the **Caffè Capitolino** (p35) is a refined spot for a restorative coffee.

Ancient ruins at the Roman Forum (p26)

❶ Colosseum

More than any other monument, it's the **Colosseum** (p24) that symbolises the power and glory of ancient Rome. A spectacular feat of engineering, the 50,000-seat stadium was inaugurated by Emperor Titus in AD 80 with a bloodthirsty bout of games that lasted 100 days and nights.

❷ Palatino

A short walk from the Colosseum, past the **Arco di Costantino** (p25), the **Palatino** (p31) was ancient Rome's most sought-after neighbourhood, site of the emperor's palace and home to the cream of imperial society. The evocative ruins are confusing but their grandeur gives some sense of the luxury in which the ancient VIPs liked to live.

❸ Roman Forum

Coming down from the Palatino you'll enter the **Roman Forum** (p26) near the **Arco di Tito** (p28), one of Rome's great triumphal arches. In imperial times, the Forum was the empire's nerve centre, a teeming hive of law courts, temples, piazzas and shops. The vestal virgins lived here and senators debated matters of state in the **Curia** (p27).

❹ Piazza del Campidoglio

Leave the Forum and climb up to the Michelangelo-designed **Piazza del Campidoglio** (p31). This striking piazza, one of Rome's most beautiful, sits atop the Campidoglio (Capitoline hill), one of the seven hills on which Rome was founded. In ancient times this was the spiritual heart of the city, home to two of the city's most important temples.

❺ Capitoline Museums

Flanking Piazza del Campidoglio are two stately *palazzi* (mansions) that together house the **Capitoline Museums** (p31). These, the world's oldest public museums, boast an important picture gallery and a superb collection of classical sculpture that includes an iconic Etruscan bronze of a wolf, the *Lupa Capitolina,* standing over Romulus and Remus.

❻ Il Vittoriano

From the Campidoglio, pop next door to the massive mountain of white marble that is **Il Vittoriano** (p32). No emperor ever walked here, but it's worth stopping off to take the panoramic lift to the top, from where you can see the whole of Rome laid out beneath you.

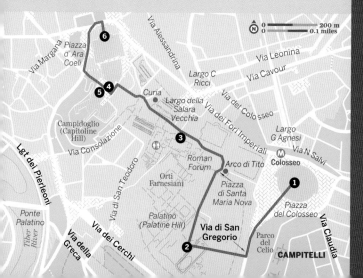

Best Walks
Piazzas of Rome

🏃 The Walk

Rome's tightly packed historic centre boasts some of the city's most celebrated piazzas, and several beautiful but lesser known squares. Each has its own character – the baroque splendour of Piazza Navona, the bawdy clamour of Campo de' Fiori, the Renaissance elegance of Piazza Farnese – but together they encapsulate much of the city's beauty, history and drama. Take this tour to discover the best of them and enjoy the area's vibrant street life.

Start Largo di Torre Argentina; 🚌 Largo di Torre Argentina

Finish Piazza Farnese; 🚌 Corso Vittorio Emanuele II

Length 1.5km; three hours

✕ Take a Break

Between the Pantheon and Piazza Navona, **Caffè Sant'Eustachio** (p50) is a good bet for a quick pit stop. Its coffee is reckoned by many to be the best in Rome.

Street vendors in Piazza Navona (p44)

❶ Largo di Torre Argentina

Start off in **Largo di Torre Argentina**, set around the ruins of four Republic-era temples. On the piazza's western flank, the **Teatro Argentina** (p52), Rome's premier theatre, sits near the site where Julius Caesar was assassinated.

❷ Piazza della Minerva

Head along Via dei Cestari until you come to **Piazza della Minerva** and the **Elefantino**, a sculpture of a puzzled elephant carrying an Egyptian obelisk. Flanking the square, the Gothic **Basilica di Santa Maria Sopra Minerva** (p45) boasts Renaissance frescoes and a minor Michelangelo.

❸ Piazza di Sant'Ignazio Loyola

Strike off down Via Santa Caterina da Siena, then take Via del Piè di Marmo and Via di Sant'Ignazio to reach the exquisite 18th-century **Piazza di Sant'Ignazio Loyola**. Overlooking the piazza, the **Chiesa di Sant'Ignazio di Loyola** (p45) features a magical trompe l'œil ceiling fresco.

❹ Piazza della Rotonda

A short stroll down Via del Seminario brings you to the bustling **Piazza della Rotonda**, where the **Pantheon** (p38) needs no introduction. Rome's best-preserved ancient building is one of the city's iconic sights with its epic portico and dome.

❺ Piazza Navona

From the Pantheon, follow the signs to **Piazza Navona** (p44), central Rome's great showpiece square. Here, among the street artists, tourists and pigeons, you can compare the two giants of Roman baroque – Gian Lorenzo Bernini, creator of the **Fontana dei Quattro Fiumi**, and Francesco Borromini, author of the **Chiesa di Sant'Agnese in Agone**.

❻ Campo de' Fiori

On the other side of Corso Vittorio Emanuele II, the busy road that bisects the *centro storico* (historic centre), life is focused on **Campo de' Fiori** (p46). By day, this noisy square stages a colourful market, at night it transforms into a raucous open-air pub.

❼ Piazza Farnese

Just beyond the Campo, **Piazza Farnese** is a refined square overlooked by the Renaissance **Palazzo Farnese** (p46). This magnificent *palazzo*, now home to the French embassy, boasts some superb frescoes, said by some to rival those of the Sistine Chapel.

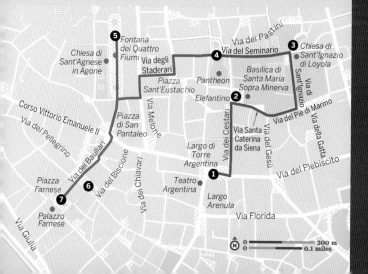

Best
History

For thousands of years Rome was at the centre of world events. First, as *caput mundi* (capital of the world), the glittering hub of the vast Roman Empire, and then as the seat of papal power. It was a city that counted and this is writ large on its historic streets, where every *palazzo*, church and ancient ruin has a tale to tell.

CHRIS MELLOR/GETTY IMAGES ©

Ancient Glories

Many of Rome's most thrilling monuments hark back to its golden age as capital of the mighty Roman Empire. The Colosseum, the Pantheon, the Roman Forum – these epic ruins all tell of past glories in a way that no textbook ever can, evoking images of teeming crowds and gladiatorial combat, pagan ceremonies and daily drama.

The Church Rules

For much of its history, the Church called the shots in Rome and many of the city's top sights are religious in origin. Early basilicas stand testament to the tenacity of the Church's founding fathers, while the masterpieces that litter the city's churches testify to the wealth and ambition of the Renaissance and baroque popes.

Multilayered History

One of Rome's characteristic features is the way that history quite literally rises from the ground. Over the centuries the city has undergone several transformations and with each one a new layer was added to the city's urban fabric. As a result, medieval churches stand over pagan temples and baroque piazzas sit atop Roman arenas. In Rome, to travel back in time you merely have to go underground.

Best Roman Relics

Colosseum Rome's iconic arena embodies all the drama of the ancient city. (p24)

Pantheon This awe-inspiring building has served as an architectural blueprint for millenniums. (p38)

Roman Forum The inspiring ruins of ancient Rome's bustling city centre. (p26)

Palatino Ancient emperors languished in luxury on the Palatino, imperial Rome's oldest and most exclusive neighbourhood. (p31)

Terme di Caracalla The towering remains of this ancient leisure centre are among Rome's most impressive. (p111)

Best for Going Underground

Basilica di San Clemente This medieval basilica sits over a pagan temple and 1st-century house. (p101)

Catacombs The Appian Way (Via Appia Antica) is riddled with catacombs where the early Christians buried their dead. (p94)

Case Romane Head underground to explore the houses where apostles John and Paul supposedly lived. (p102)

Museo Nazionale Romano: Crypta Balbi A museum atop Renaissance ruins atop a 1st-century-BC theatre. (p46)

Best Historical Churches

St Peter's Basilica The Vatican's monumental showpiece church stands over St Peter's tomb. (p136; pictured left)

Basilica di San Giovanni in Laterano The main papal basilica until the 14th century. (p98)

Basilica di San Paolo Fuori le Mura Monumental basilica on the site where St Paul was buried. (p107)

Chiesa del Gesù Important Jesuit church, home to Ignatius Loyola for 12 years. (p44)

Best for Legends

Palatino Where the wolf saved Romulus and Remus, and Rome was founded in 753 BC. (p31)

Bocca della Verità Tell a lie and the 'Mouth of Truth' will bite your hand off. (p33)

Basilica di San Pietro in Vincoli Houses the miraculous chains that bound St Peter. (p85)

Trevi Fountain Throw a coin in and you'll return to Rome. (p68)

Teatro Argentina Rome's top theatre overlooks the site where Julius Caesar was assassinated. (p52)

Chiesa di Santa Maria del Popolo Was supposedly built to exorcise Nero's malicious spirit which haunted the area. (p59)

Worth a Trip

Rome's answer to Pompeii, the **Scavi Archeologici di Ostia Antica** (Archaeological Excavations of Ostia Antica; ☎06 5635 0215; www.ostiaantica.beniculturali. it; Viale dei Romagnoli 717; adult/reduced €10/6; ⏰8.30am-6.15pm Tue-Sun summer, earlier closing winter) offer a well-preserved insight into ancient Rome's once-thriving port. Highlights include the Terme di Nettuno and the impressive amphitheatre. To get to the site take the suburban train to Ostia Antica from Stazione Porta San Paolo next to Piramide metro station.

Best
Food

Food is central to the Roman passion for life. Everyone has an opinion on it and the city teems with trattorias, pizzerias, fine-dining restaurants and gourmet gelaterie. Traditional Roman cooking holds sway but *cucina creativa* (creative cooking) has taken off in recent years and there are plenty of exciting, contemporary restaurants to try.

LISA KYLE YOUNG/GETTY IMAGES ©

The Traditional Trattoria

The bedrock of the Roman food scene has always been the family-run trattorias that pepper the city's streets and piazzas. These simple eateries, often with rickety wooden tables and *nonna* (grandma) at the stove, have been feeding visitors for centuries and are still the best bet for hearty, no-nonsense Roman dishes such as *bucatini all'amatriciana* (thick spaghetti with tomato sauce and *guanciale* – cured pig's cheek) or *spaghetti alla gricia* (with pancetta and *pecorino* – sheep's milk cheese).

Contemporary Fine Dining

Over recent decades Rome's restaurant scene has become increasingly sophisticated with new-wave trattorias and chic designer restaurants offering edgy, innovative food. Leading the way, Cristina Bowerman of Glass Hostaria and Giuseppe Di Iorio of Aroma have made their names with their modern, creative approach to Italian cuisine.

Street Food

The latest foodie fad to hit Rome is a passion for street food. Alongside the many *pizza al taglio* (sliced pizza) joints and gelaterie, a host of hip new places have opened across town serving classic snacks such as *supplì* (fried rice balls with various fillings) and *fritti* (fried foods) with a modern twist.

☑ **Top Tips**

▶ In a trattoria or restaurant, you'll be given bread and charged for it whether you eat it or not. This is standard practice, not a tourist rip-off.

▶ For water, ask for *acqua naturale* (still) or *acqua frizzante* (sparkling).

▶ Round the bill up in a pizzeria or trattoria in lieu of a tip; leave up to 10% in a more upmarket restaurant.

PAOLO CIPRIANI/GETTY IMAGES ©

Restaurant menu showing daily specials

Best Fine Dining

Glass Hostaria Wonderful, innovative food in a contemporary setting in Trastevere. (p125)

Open Colonna Chef Antonello Colonna's glassroofed restaurant offers creative takes on Roman classics. (p87)

Aroma Beautiful setting, and chef Giuseppe Di Iorio bedazzles with forward-thinking Mediterranean cuisine. (p103)

Imàgo Haute cuisine and haute views from the rooftop restaurant of the five-star Hassler Hotel. (p61)

Best Roman

Flavio al Velavevodetto A relaxed Testaccio trattoria serving excellent Roman fare. (p112)

Armando al Pantheon A bastion of Roman cuisine in the touristy Pantheon area. (p47)

Enoteca Regionale Palatium Sleek wine bar showcasing food from the Lazio region. (p60)

Ristorante L'Arcangelo Superlative Roman staples at this perennial Prati favourite. (p143)

Pizzeria Da Remo Serves up thin-crust Roman-style pizzas and a boisterous atmosphere. (p113)

Best Fast Food

Pizzarium Near the Vatican Museums, this is the best pizza takeaway in town. (p142)

Supplizio Gourmet versions of Rome's favourite fried risotto ball snacks, *supplì*. (p47)

Forno Roscioli A seriously good bakery-cum-deli in the historic centre. (p49)

Trapizzino Home of the *trapizzino*, a cone of doughy bread stuffed with a saucy filler. (p113)

Best Gelato

Fatamorgana Rome's finest artisanal flavours, now in multiple locations. (p60)

Il Gelato Taste the experimental ice creams of Claudio Torcè, Rome's gelato king. (p113)

Dei Gracchi A taste of heaven in several locations across Rome. (p62)

Venchi Specialises in all things chocolaty. (p49)

Best For Free

Although Rome is an expensive city, you don't have to break the bank to enjoy it. A surprising number of its big sights are free, including all churches, and it costs nothing to stroll the historic streets, piazzas and parks, basking in their extraordinary beauty.

JAMES HARDY/GETTY IMAGES ©

Best Places for Free Art

St Peter's Basilica Michelangelo's *Pietà* is just one of the masterpieces on display. (p136)

Basilica di San Pietro in Vincoli Feast your eyes on Michelangelo's fearsome *Moses*. (p85)

Chiesa di San Luigi dei Francesi Caravaggio's St Matthew cycle is the big drawcard here. (p44)

Chiesa di Santa Maria del Popolo Works by Caravaggio, Raphael and Bernini adorn this Renaissance church. (p59)

Chiesa di Santa Maria della Vittoria Features Bernini's astonishing *Ecstasy of St Teresa*, a seminal baroque work. (p71)

Vatican Museums Free on the last Sunday of each month. (p132)

Best Piazzas & Parks

Piazza Navona A colourful cast of street artists create a carnival atmosphere on this stunning baroque piazza. (p44)

Campo de' Fiori Revel in the chaos of the Campo's daily market. (p46)

Piazza del Popolo Sit under the central obelisk and watch the world go by. (p59)

Villa Borghese Rome's central park is ideal for leisurely strolling and picnics. (p1476)

Gianicolo Admire magnificent views from this leafy hill. (p120)

Best Free Monuments

Pantheon It doesn't cost a penny to enter this extraordinary church. (p38)

☑ Top Tips

▶ All state-run museums and sites are free on the first Sunday of the month.

▶ Save a few euros by filling up with water from drinking fountains known as *nasoni* (big noses) dotted around the streets.

Trevi Fountain Throw a coin into the fountain to ensure your return to Rome. (p68)

Bocca della Verità Test the legend – tell a lie with your hand in the mouth. (p33; pictured above)

Spanish Steps Grab a perch and hang out on Rome's most celebrated staircase. (p56)

Best
Bars & Nightlife

Nightlife in Rome is all about enjoying the vibe and lapping up the spectacular surroundings. The city's central streets buzz well into the night as locals crowd into popular bars and cafes before heading off late to a club. Clubbing action caters to most tastes, with DJs spinning everything from lounge and jazz to house, dancehall and hip hop.

GARY YEOWELL/GETTY IMAGES ©

Best Areas

Centro Storico Bars and a few clubs, a mix of tourists and locals of all ages. (p50)

Trastevere Everyone's favourite evening hangout, with plenty of bars and cafes. (p120)

Testaccio A nightlife hotspot with a parade of crowd-pleasing clubs on Monte Testaccio. (p114)

Ostiense Home to Rome's grittier clubs, many housed in ex-industrial venues. (p106)

San Lorenzo & Pigneto Fashionable bars and alternative clubs draw students, bohemians and hipsters. (p78)

Best Bars & Cafes

Barnum Cafe A cool *centro storico* bar with vintage decor, a laid-back vibe, and top cocktails. (p50)

Sciascia Caffè A polished Prati cafe that serves superlative coffee. (p144)

Co.So A buzzing Pigneto hot spot known for its trend-setting cocktails. (p79)

Ma Che Siete Venuti a Fà Quaff craft beers at this tiny Trastevere pub. (p126)

Caffè Sant'Eustachio Unglamorous cafe that serves some of the capital's best coffee. (p50)

Best Clubs

Goa A historic Ostiense club featuring top international DJs and a fashion-forward crowd. (p107)

 Top Tips

▶ Take your cue from the locals and dress up to go out, particularly in the *centro storico* (historic centre) and Testaccio.

▶ Some popular clubs have a seemingly whimsical door policy, and men, single or in groups, are often turned away.

▶ Events are often listed for 10pm but don't kick off until around 11pm; clubs rarely hot up until after 1am.

ConteStaccio One of the best venues on the Testaccio clubbing strip. (p115)

Best
Architecture

Boasting ancient ruins, Renaissance basilicas, baroque churches and hulking fascist *palazzi*, Rome's architectural legacy is unparalleled. Michelangelo, Bramante, Borromini and Bernini are among the architects who have stamped their genius on its remarkable cityscape, while in recent times a number of the world's top architects have completed projects in the city.

Ancient Engineering

In building the *caput mundi* (capital of the world), ancient Rome's architects and engineers were called on to design houses, roads, aqueducts and shopping centres alongside temples, tombs and imperial palaces. To do so they advanced methods devised by the Etruscans and Greeks and developed construction techniques that allowed them to build on a hitherto unseen scale.

Renaissance & Baroque Makeovers

Many of Rome's great *palazzi* and basilicas date to the Renaissance 16th century, including St Peter's Basilica, which was given a complete overhaul by Bramante, Michelangelo et al. A century later, the Counter-Reformation paved the way for a Church-sponsored makeover led by the baroque heroes Gian Lorenzo Bernini and Francesco Borromini.

Modern Architecture

In the early 20th century, Italy's Fascist dictator Benito Mussolini oversaw a number of grandiose building projects, including Via dei Fori Imperiali and the EUR district. More recently, projects have been completed by a roll-call of top international 'starchitects' including Renzo Piano, Massimiliano Fuksas, Richard Meier and Zaha Hadid.

Best Ancient Monuments

Colosseum A blueprint for modern stadiums, Rome's gladiatorial arena dramatically illustrates the use of the arch. (p24)

Pantheon The ancient Romans' greatest architectural achievement was revolutionary in both design and execution. (p38)

Terme di Caracalla These looming ruins hint at the sophistication of ancient building techniques. (p111)

Mercati di Traiano Museo dei Fori Imperiali A towering model of 2nd-century civic engineering. (p32)

Best Early Basilicas

Basilica di San Giovanni in Laterano Its original design was the blueprint for basilicas to follow. (p98)

Basilica di Santa Maria Maggiore The only one of Rome's four patriarchal basilicas to retain its original layout. (p85)

Basilica di Santa Sabina This medieval gem sports an austere, no-frills basilica look. (p111)

Basilica di Santa Maria in Trastevere Ancient Roman columns and glittering mosaics feature in this Trastevere highlight. (p118)

Best Renaissance Buildings

Tempietto di Bramante Bramante's influential masterpiece of harmonious design encapsulates High Renaissance ideals. (p123)

St Peter's Basilica An amalgamation of designs, styles and plans, capped by Michelangelo's extraordinary dome. (p136)

Palazzo Farnese Home to the French embassy, this is a fine example of a Renaissance palace. (p46)

Piazza del Campidoglio Michelangelo's hilltop piazza is a show-stopping model of Renaissance town planning. (p31)

Best Baroque Gems

St Peter's Square Bernini designed the Vatican's focal square to funnel believers into St Peter's Basilica. (p142)

Piazza Navona With a Borromini church and a Bernini fountain, this square is a model of baroque beauty. (p44)

Chiesa di San Carlo alle Quattro Fontane Borromini's petite church

bears many of his trademark tricks. (p71)

Chiesa di Sant'Andrea al Quirinale One of Bernini's finest architectural works. (p72)

Best Modern Icons

Palazzo della Civiltà del Lavoro (pictured left) Known as the Square Colosseum, this *palazzo* is typical of 1930s rationalism.

Auditorium Parco della Musica Renzo Piano's avant-garde concert complex features a unique architectural design. (p148)

Museo dell'Ara Pacis Controversially designed by Richard Meier, this white pavilion houses an important 1st-century-BC altar. (p59)

MAXXI Zaha Hadid's converted barracks houses Rome's top contemporary art museum. (p148)

Worth a Trip

One of the few planned developments in Rome's history, the **Esposizione Universale di Roma** (Roman Universal Exhibition; EUR) area was built for an international exhibition in 1942. There are a few museums, but the area's interest lies in its spectacular rationalist architecture – best expressed in the iconic **Palazzo della Civiltà del Lavoro** (Quadrato della Concordia; M EUR Magliana).

Best
Art & Museums

Home to some of the Western world's greatest art, Rome is a visual feast. Its churches contain more masterpieces than many small countries and its museums and galleries are laden with instantly recognisable works. From classical statues and stunning Renaissance frescoes to breathtaking baroque sculptures and futuristic paintings, the art on show spans almost 3000 years of artistic endeavour.

Classical Art

Not surprisingly, Rome's collection of ancient art – largely comprising sculpture, commemorative reliefs, and mosaics – is unparalleled. The Vatican Museums and Capitoline Museums showcase much of the city's finest classical sculpture but you'll also find superlative pieces in Palazzo Altemps and Palazzo Massimo alle Terme.

The Renaissance

The Renaissance unleashed an artistic maelstrom in Rome as powerful Church patrons commissioned artists such as Michelangelo and Raphael to decorate the city's basilicas and palaces. Fresco painting was a key endeavour and many celebrated frescoes date to this period, including Michelangelo's Sistine Chapel designs (in the Vatican Museums).

The Baroque

The baroque burst onto Rome's art scene in the early 17th century and was enthusiastically adopted by the Church as a propaganda tool in its battle against Reformation heresy. Works by the period's two leading artists – Gian Lorenzo Bernini and controversial painter Caravaggio – adorn churches and museums across the city.

☑ Top Tips

▶ Most museums are closed on Mondays.

▶ EU citizens under 18 often qualify for free admission. Take ID as proof of age.

▶ All state-run museums are free on the first Sunday of the month.

▶ Many museums close their ticket offices up to 75 minutes before closing time.

Modern Art

The 20th century saw the emergence of futurism, a nationalistic modernist movement, and metaphysical painting, an Italian form of surrealism best expressed in the works of Giorgio de Chirico.

Best Museums & Galleries

Vatican Museums
The Sistine Chapel and Raphael Rooms headline at this spectacular museum complex. (p132)

Museo e Galleria Borghese Houses Rome's best baroque sculpture and some superlative Old Masters. (p147)

Capitoline Museums
Ancient sculpture is the main draw at the world's oldest public museums. (p31)

Museo Nazionale Romano: Palazzo Massimo alle Terme An overlooked gem boasting fabulous Roman sculpture and mosaics. (p82)

Museo Nazionale Romano: Palazzo Altemps Blazing baroque frescoes provide the background for classical sculpture. (p44)

Galleria Doria Pamphilj
A lavish gallery full of major works by big-name artists. (p44)

Best Masterpieces

Sistine Chapel Home to Michelangelo's celebrated ceiling frescoes and *Giudizio universale* (Last Judgment). (p134)

Pietà A work of sculptural genius and a highlight of St Peter's Basilica. (p137)

La Scuola di Atene The greatest of Raphael's frescoes in the Stanze di Raffaello (Vatican Museums). (p134)

Santa Teresa trafitta dall'amore di dio The Chiesa di Santa Maria della Vittoria is home to this Bernini sculpture, one of the masterpieces of European baroque art. (p71)

Ratto di Proserpina
Another Bernini sculpture, this one depicting Pluto abducting Proserpina, at the Museo e Galleria Borghese. (p147)

Ragazzo col canestro di frutta Admire Caravaggio's technical mastery and fearless bravado in the Museo e Galleria Borghese. (p147)

Trionfo della divina provvidenza Head to the Galleria Nazionale d'Arte Antica: Palazzo Barberini for Pietro da Cortona's *Triumph of Divine Providence*. (p71)

Best Little-Known Gems

Museo Nazionale Etrusco di Villa Giulia
Italy's premier Etruscan museum. (p147)

Castel Sant'Angelo Admire lavish Renaissance interiors in this brooding landmark castle. (p142)

Mercati di Traiano Museo dei Fori Imperiali A museum set in Trajan's towering 2nd-century shopping mall. (p32)

Centrale Montemartini
A former power station juxtaposes ancient sculpture with industrial machinery. (p107)

Best Modern Art

Galleria Nazionale d'Arte Moderna e Contemporanea Study works by the giants of modern European art. (p148)

MAXXI Rome's premier contemporary arts museum. (p148)

Museo Carlo Bilotti
Boasts a collection of metaphysical paintings by Giorgio de Chirico. (p148)

Best
Shopping

Rome boasts the usual cast of flagship chain stores and glitzy designer outlets, but what makes shopping here so special is its legion of small, independent shops – historic, family-owned delis, picture-framers, dusty furniture workshops, small-label fashion boutiques and artists' studios. Adding to the fun are the much-frequented neighbourhood markets selling everything from secondhand jeans to bumper produce from local farms.

What to Buy

Rome is a top place to shop for designer clothes, shoes and leather goods. Foodie treats are another obvious choice and you'll find no end of delis, bakeries, *pasticcerie* (pastry shops) and chocolate shops. Homeware is another Italian speciality, and many shops focus on covetable kitchenware and sleek interior design.

Shopping Areas

For designer clothes head to Via dei Condotti and the area around Piazza di Spagna. You'll find vintage shops and fashion boutiques on Via del Governo Vecchio in the *centro storico,* and in the Monti district. Testaccio is a good bet for foodie purchases, with one of Rome's best delis and a daily market.

Artisans

Rome has a surprising number of designers and artisans, who create and sell their goods in small, old-fashioned workshops. There are places you can get a bag, wallet or belt made to your specifications, or order a tailored tie or dress. You'll find a number of these in the *centro storico,* Tridente and Monti areas.

INGOLF POMPE/GETTY IMAGES ©

☑ **Top Tips**

▶ Many shops are closed on Monday morning.

▶ Take the receipt when you buy something.

▶ Tax rebates are available to non-EU residents who spend more than €175 in shops displaying a Tax Free sticker.

▶ Winter sales (*saldi*) run from early January to mid-February; summer sales from July to early September.

Porta Portese market (p128), Trastevere

Best Fashion

Tina Sondergaard
Handmade retro fashions at this popular Monti boutique. (p90)

101 A Monti boutique specialising in gorgeous women's designs and accessories. (p91)

Fendi The flagship store of the Rome-born fashion brand. (p64)

SBU Hip store for cool-cut jeans. (p41)

Luna & L'Altra Fashion-heaven, with clothes by Comme des Garçons, Issey Miyake and Yohji Yamamoto. (p53)

Best Shoes & Accessories

Borini Locals head to this low-key shop for the latest shoes. (p53)

Danielle Fashionable women's shoes, in a rainbow palette of colours, at affordable prices. (p64)

Pelletteria Nives Have a leather bag made to your specifications. (p65)

La Cravatta su Misura Bespoke ties for the well-groomed modern gentleman. (p128)

Best Food & Wine

Volpetti Foodies rate this lavish deli as one of the best in town. (p115)

Confetteria Moriondo & Gariglio A historic chocolate shop straight out of central casting. (p52)

Enoteca Costantini One of Rome's best-stocked wine shops with a huge collection of international labels. (p145)

Antica Caciara Trasteverina A Trastevere deli celebrated for its fab cheeses. (p128)

Best Markets

Porta Portese Rome's historic Sunday-morning flea market on the banks of the Tiber. (p128)

Nuovo Mercato di Testaccio Enjoy colours and characters at Testaccio's neighbourhood market. (p115)

Campo de' Fiori One of Rome's best-known markets on a historic central piazza. (p46)

Best
Culture

The Romans have long been passionate about culture. Ever since crowds flocked to the Colosseum for gladiatorial games, the locals have enjoyed a good show, and cultural events draw knowledgable and enthusiastic audiences. And with everything from opera to hip hop, Shakespearian drama and avant-garde installations on the program, you're sure to find a style to suit.

Opera & Classical Music

Rome's abundance of beautiful settings makes it a wonderful place to catch a concert. Classical music performances – often free – are regularly held in churches, especially around Easter, Christmas and the New Year, while summer sees stages set up in outdoor locations across the city. Top venues, such as the Auditorium Parco della Musica, often host big-name Italian and international orchestras and performers.

Film, Drama & Exhibitions

Romans are great cinema-goers and although most films are dubbed you can still catch a movie in its original language (marked VO in listings – *versione originale*). Similarly, theatres tend to stage performances in Italian, but you might strike it lucky. You'll have no language problems enjoying the many art exhibitions that come to town.

Centri Sociali & Counterculture

Rome's alternative scene is focused on the city's *centri sociali* (social centres). These counterculture hubs, which started life as organised squats, gave rise to Italy's hip-hop and rap scenes in the 1980s and still stage alternative entertainment, be it poetry slams, indie fashion shows or drum-and-bass gigs.

MAXIM APRYATIN/SHUTTERSTOCK ©

☑ Top Tips

▶ Look for upcoming events at www.060608.it, www.auditorium.com and www.inromenow.com.

▶ Check for events staged during Rome's arts festivals, particularly in summer and autumn.

Best for Classical Music & Opera

Auditorium Parco della Musica Rome's premier concert venue and cultural centre. (p148; pictured above)

Teatro dell'Opera di Roma Rome's opera house, home to the city's opera and ballet companies. (p89)

Terme di Caracalla
Haunting ancient ruins
provide the spellbinding
backdrop for summer
opera and ballet. (p111)

Teatro Olimpico Stages
classical music, ballet,
opera and more modern
offerings.

Best for Jazz & Blues

Alexanderplatz Top
international artists lead
the way at Rome's his-
toric jazz club. (p145)

Big Mama Blues and
jazz rule the roost at this
Trastevere basement
club. (p121)

Gregory's Much-loved
jazz club frequented by
local musicians. (p77)

Charity Café An intimate
venue hosting regular
jazz in Monti. (p90)

Lettere Caffè Gallery A
cool, booky venue host-
ing live jazz and a wide
range of cultural events.
(p127)

Best for Live Gigs

ConteStaccio Catch
everything from extreme
electro to U2 tribute
bands at this Testaccio
club. (p115)

Blackmarket Bar filled
with vintage sofas and
armchairs, great for
eclectic, mainly acoustic
live music. (p90)

Fonclea This Prati pub
sets the stage for soul,
jazz, rock and Latin.
(p145)

Best Exhibition Spaces

**Palazzo delle Espo-
sizioni** This neoclassical
cultural centre often
hosts big international
exhibitions. (p86)

**Scuderie Papali al
Quirinale** A wonderful
gallery housed in the
pope's former stables.
(p72)

MAXXI Rome's contem-
porary arts hub stages
avant-garde exhibitions
and installations. (p148)

Chiostro del Bramante
Renaissance cloisters
set the scene for popular
temporary exhibitions.
(p40)

Best Theatres

Teatro Argentina Home
of the Teatro di Roma,
Rome's top theatre offers
a wide-ranging program.
(p52)

Ostia Antica Summer
theatre is staged in an
ancient amphitheatre
built by Agrippa. (p157)

Best for a Film

Nuovo Sacher Film
director Nanni Moretti
oversees the program at
this, his personal cinema.
(p121)

Worth a Trip

While the star attraction at the **Teatro Olimpico** (☏ 06 326 59 91; www.
teatroolimpico.it; Piazza Gentile da Fabriano 17; 🚇 Piazza Mancini, 🚇 Piazza Mancini) is the
season of classical music by the in-house **Accademia Filarmonica Romana**
(www.filarmonicaromana.org), Rome's Olympic Theatre also stages opera, ballet,
one-man shows, contemporary gigs and comedies. It's in the Flaminio district,
northwest of Villa Borghese.

Best
For Kids

STEFAN CIOATA/GETTY IMAGES ©

Despite a reputation as a highbrow cultural destination, Rome has a lot to offer kids. Child-specific sights might be thin on the ground, but if you know where to go there's plenty to keep the little 'uns occupied. And with so much pizza and gelato on the menu, meal times should be a breeze.

Explora – Museo dei Bambini di Roma (✆06 361 37 76; www.mdbr.it; Via Flaminia 82; adult/reduced €8/5; ⏲entry times 10am, noon, 3pm & 5pm Tue-Sun; Ⓜ Flaminio) Rome's only dedicated kids museum is aimed at the under-12s. It's divided into thematic sections and with everything from a supermarket to a play pool and fire engine, it's a hands-on, feet-on, full-on experience that your nippers will love. Bookings recommended and essential at weekends.

Museo delle Cere (✆06 679 64 82; www. museodellecereroma. com; Piazza dei Santissimi Apostoli 67; adult/reduced €9/7; ⏲9am-9pm; 🚌Via IV Novembre) Rome's waxwork museum is said to have the world's third-largest collection, which comprises more than 250 figures, ranging from Barack Obama to Snow White, plus plentiful other popes, poets, politicians, musicians and murderers.

Bioparco (✆06 360 82 11; www.bioparco.it; Viale del Giardino Zoologico 1; adult/reduced €15/12; ⏲9.30am-6pm summer, to 5pm winter; 🚌Bioparco) A reliable kid-friendly choice, Rome's zoo hosts a predictable collection of animals, including lions, tigers, giraffes and monkeys, on an 18-hectare site in Villa Borghese.

Best
Tours

Best Walking

A Friend in Rome

(📞340 501 92 01; www.
afriendinrome.it) Silvia
Prosperi organises
private tailor-made
tours (on foot, by bike
or scooter) to suit your
interests. She covers the
Vatican and main historic
centre as well as areas
outside the capital. Rates
are €50 per hour, with a
minimum of three hours
for most tours.

The Roman Guy (www.the

romanguy.com) Organises
a wide range of group and
private tours. Packages,
led by English-speaking
experts, include early-
bird visits to the Vatican
Museums, foodie tours
of Trastevere and the
Jewish Ghetto, and a bar
hop through the historic
centre's cocktail bars.

Best by Bus

Open Bus Cristiana

(www.operaromana
pellegrinaggi.org; single
tour €15, 24/48hr ticket
€20/48; ⊗9am-6pm)
A hop-on, hop-off bus
departing from Via della
Conciliazione and Ter-
mini. Stops are situated
near to main sights
including St Peter's
Basilica, Piazza Navona,
the Trevi Fountain and
the Colosseum. Tickets
are available on board or
at the meeting point just
off St Peter's Square.

Best by Bike or
Scooter

Top Bike Rental &

Tours (📞06 488 28 93;
www.topbikerental.com; Via
Labicana 49; ⊗10am-7pm)
Offers a series of bike
tours throughout the
city, including a four-hour

GUY THOUVENIN/GETTY IMAGES ©

16km exploration of the
city centre (€45) and
an all-day 30km ride
through the Appian Way
and environs (€79).

Bici & Baci (📞06 482 84
43; www.bicibaci.com; Via
del Viminale 5; ⊗8am-7pm)
Bici & Baci runs daily
bike tours of central
Rome, taking in the his-
toric centre, Campidoglio
and the Colosseum, as
well as tours on vintage
Vespas and in classic Fiat
500 cars. Reckon on €49
for the bike tour, €145 for
the Vespa ride and €290
for the four-hour guided
drive.

Best
Gay & Lesbian

Rome has a thriving, if low-key, gay scene. The big annual events, including the summer-long Gay Village and Roma Pride, are colourful crowd-pleasers. There are relatively few queer-only venues but the Colosseum end of Via di San Giovanni in Laterano is a favourite hangout and many of the city's top clubs host regular gay and lesbian nights.

HUW JONES/GETTY IMAGES ©

Attitudes

Rome is by nature a conservative city and its legislators have long looked to the Vatican for guidance on moral and social issues. That said, the city's gay community has taken steps out of the closet in recent times and while Rome is no San Fran on the Med, and discretion is still wise, tolerance is widespread.

Gay Village

Rome's big annual event is **Gay Village** (www.gay village.it), held between June and September in EUR (although the location changes, so check ahead). Attracting huge crowds and an exuberant cast of DJs, musicians and entertainers, it serves up an eclectic mix of dance music, film screenings, cultural debates, theatrical performances, and, for sports fans, the Italian Gaymes.

Best Gay Venues

Coming Out A welcoming bar near the Colosseum that hots up in the evening. (p104)

L'Alibi On the Testaccio clubbing strip, an ever-popular gay (but not exclusively so) club. (p115)

☑ **Top Tips**

▶ Many gay venues ask for the Arcigay Card (€15), available on the door if required.

▶ For local information, pick up the monthly magazine *AUT*, published by **Circolo Mario Mieli** (☎ 800 110611; www. mariomieli.org; Via Efeso 2a). Other resources include **AZ Gay** (www. azgay.it), and **Coordinamento Lesbiche Italiano** (www.clrbp. it; Via San Francesco di Sales 1b).

Survival Guide

Before You Go   174

When to Go...................... 174

Book Your Stay.................... 174

Arriving in Rome   176

Leonardo da Vinci Airport (Fiumicino) 176

Ciampino Airport 176

Stazione Termini & Bus Station 177

Getting Around   177

Metro........................... 177

Bus............................. 178

Tram............................ 178

Taxi............................ 178

Train 179

Essential Information   179

Business Hours.................... 179

Discount Cards.................... 179

Electricity 180

Emergencies...................... 180

Money 180

Public Holidays 181

Safe Travel...................... 181

Telephone Services 181

Toilets 182

Tourist Information 182

Travellers with Disabilities 183

Visas........................... 183

Language   184

Survival Guide

Before You Go

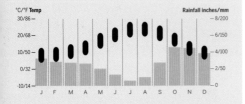

When to Go

°C/°F Temp
30/86 —
20/68 —
10/50 —
0/32 —
-10/14 —

Rainfall inches/mm
— 8/200
— 6/150
— 4/100
— 2/50
— 0

J F M A M J J A S O N D

➡ **Winter (Dec–Feb)**
Cold, short days.
Museums are quiet and
prices are low except at
Christmas and New Year.

➡ **Spring (Mar–May)**
Warm, sunny weather.
Fervent Easter celebra-
tions and azaleas on the
Spanish Steps. Busy and
high prices.

➡ **Summer (Jun–Aug)**
Very hot. Plenty of out-
door events. In August,
Romans desert the city
and hoteliers drop prices.

➡ **Autumn (Sep–Nov)**
Still warm. Crowds die
down and the Ro-
maeuropa festival is on.
November brings rain
and low-season prices.

Book Your Stay

☑ When reserving a room,
ask for a *camera matrimo-
niale* if you want a double
bed, or a *camera doppia*
for twin beds.

➡ Accommodation runs
the gamut from five-star
palaces and designer
guesthouses to family-
run *pensioni* (small ho-
tels), B&Bs and tranquil
convents.

➡ Book in the *centro
storico* (historic centre)
for the best atmosphere,
though rates are high and
rooms can be noisy.

➡ Other areas: Trastevere
is good for party people
and deep sleepers.
Termini is full of hostels
and budget *pensioni*, but
isn't Rome's prettiest
neighbourhood. Prati is
quiet and well-connected
near the Vatican. Tridente

is full of designer shops, boutique guesthouses and luxury five-stars.

➡ Rooms in Rome tend to be small, even in top-end places.

➡ Rates are universally high. They're at their lowest from November to March (excluding Christmas and New Year) and from mid-July through August. Expect to pay top whack in spring (April to June) and autumn (September and October) and over the main holiday periods (Christmas, New Year and Easter).

➡ On top of rates, Rome hotels apply a room occupancy tax. This amounts to: €3 per person per night for a maximum of 10 days in one- and two-star hotels; €3.50 in B&Bs; €4/6/7 in three-/four-/five-star hotels.

Useful Websites

➡ **060608** (www.060608.it) Has a full list of accommodation options.

➡ **Lonely Planet** (www. lonelyplanet.com/rome) Check author-reviewed accommodation and book online.

➡ **Bed & Breakfast Association of Rome** (www.b-b. rm.it) Lists B&Bs and short-term apartment rentals.

➡ **Santa Susanna** (www. santasusanna.org/coming-ToRome/convents.html) Details religious institutions offering accommodation.

Best Budget

➡ **Althea Inn** (www. altheainn.com) Designer comfort at budget prices in the Testaccio area.

➡ **Beehive** (www.the-beehive.com) Boutique hostel near Termini.

➡ **Hotel Panda** (www.hotel panda.it) Long-standing favourite in the pricey Spanish Steps area.

➡ **San Pietrino** (www.san-pietrino.it) Characterful rooms in a cosy Vatican *pensione*.

Best Midrange

➡ **Palm Gallery Hotel** (www.palmgalleryhotel.com) A delightful villa hotel just east of Villa Borghese.

➡ **Residenza Maritti** (www.residenzamaritti.com) Welcoming hideaway located close to the

Roman and Imperial forums.

➡ **Arco del Lauro** (www. arcodellauro.it) A cool bolthole in happening Trastevere.

➡ **Albergo Cesàri** (www. albergocesari.it) Historic hotel in wonderful central location.

➡ **Daphne Inn** (www. daphne-rome.com) Boutique hotel with superlative service near Piazza Barberini.

Best Top End

➡ **Hotel Campo de' Fiori** (www.hotelcampodefiori.com) Baroque decor, enviable location, and professional service.

➡ **Villa Spalletti Trivelli** (www.villaspalletti.it) Glorious mansion overlooking the Quirinale gardens.

➡ **Babuino 181** (www. romeluxurysuites.com/ babuino) Discreet, modern luxury on a smart shopping street near Piazza del Popolo.

➡ **Hotel Sant'Anselmo** (www.aventinohotels.com) Romantic hideaway in the graceful Aventino district.

Arriving in Rome

....

☑ **Top Tip** For the best way to get to your accommodation, see p17.

Leonardo da Vinci Airport (Fiumicino)

➡ The easiest way to get from the airport is by train, but there are also buses and private shuttle services.

➡ The set taxi fare to/from the city centre is €48, which is valid for up to four passengers with luggage. Taxis registered in Fiumicino charge more, so make sure you catch a Comune di Roma taxi – these are white with the words *Roma Capitale* on the side along with the driver's ID number. Journey time is approximately 45 to 60 minutes.

Leonardo Express Train

(one way €14) Runs to/from Stazione Termini. Departs from the airport every 30 minutes between 6.23am and 11.23pm; from Termini between 5.35am and 10.35pm. Journey time is 30 minutes.

FL1 Train (one way €8) Connects to Trastevere, Ostiense and Tiburtina stations, but not Termini. Departures from the airport every 15 minutes (half-hourly on Sundays and public holidays) between 5.57am and 10.42pm; from Tiburtina every 15 minutes between 5.46am and 7.31pm, then half-hourly to 10.02pm.

SIT Bus (☎06 591 68 26; www.sitbusshuttle.it; one way €6) Regular departures from the airport to Stazione Termini (Via Marsala) from 8.30am to 11.50pm; from Termini between 5am and 8.30pm. All buses stop at the Vatican en route. Tickets are available on the bus. Journey time is approximately one hour.

Cotral Bus (www.cotralspa. it; one way €5, if bought on the bus €7) Runs to/from Fiumicino from Stazione Tiburtina via Termini. Eight daily departures including night services from the airport at 1.15am, 2.15am, 3.30am and 5am, and from Tiburtina at 12.30am, 1.15am, 2.30am and 3.45am. Journey time is one hour.

Airport shuttle (www.air portshuttle.it) Transfers to/from your hotel for €25 for one person, then €5 for each additional passenger up to a maximum of eight.

Ciampino Airport

➡ To get into town, the best bet is to take one of the dedicated bus services. You can also take a bus to Ciampino station and pick up a train to Stazione Termini.

➡ The set taxi rate to/from the city centre is €30. It typically takes 30 to 45 minutes.

➡ The **airport shuttle** (www.airportshuttle.it) runs transfers to/from your hotel for €25 for one person, then €5 for each additional passenger up to a maximum of eight.

Terravision Bus (www. terravision.eu; one way €6, online €4) Twice hourly departures to/from Via Marsala outside Stazione Termini. From the airport services are between 8.15am and 12.15am; from Via Marsala between 4.30am and 9.20pm. Buy tickets at Terracafè in front of the Via Marsala bus stop. Journey time is 40 minutes.

SIT Bus (✆06 591 68 26; www.sitbusshuttle.com; from/ to airport €4/6) Regular departures from the airport to Via Marsala outside Stazione Termini between 7.45am and 11.15pm; from Termini between 4.30am and 9.30pm. Get tickets on the bus. Journey time is 45 minutes.

Atral (www.atral-lazio.com) Runs buses to/from Anagnina metro station (€1.20) and Ciampino train station (€1.20), where you can get a train to Termini (€1.30).

Stazione Termini & Bus Station

➡ Stazione Termini (Map p84, D2) is Rome's main train station and transport hub, with regular connections to other European destinations, major Italian cities and many smaller towns.

➡ From Termini, you can connect onto metro lines A or B, or take a bus from the bus station on Piazza dei Cinquecento out front.

➡ Taxis line up outside the main exit/entrance. Assume about €10 to a central Rome address.

Getting Around

Rome is a sprawling city, but the historic centre is relatively compact and it's quite possible to explore much of it on foot. The city's public transport system includes buses, trams, metro and a suburban train system. Tickets, which come in various forms, are valid on all forms of transport.

Metro

☑ **Best for...** Avoiding traffic jams and for getting around quickly.

➡ Rome has two main metro lines, A (orange) and B (blue), which cross at Termini.

➡ Trains run between 5.30am and 11.30pm (to 1.30am on Fridays and Saturdays).

➡ Take line A for the Trevi Fountain (Barberini), Spanish Steps

Tickets & Passes

Public transport tickets are valid on all modes of public transit, except on trains to Leonardo da Vinci (Fiumicino) Airport.

➡ **BIT** (*biglietto integrato a tempo,* a single ticket valid for 100 minutes and one metro ride) €1.50

➡ **Roma 24h** (valid for 24 hours) €7

➡ **Roma 48h** (valid for 48 hours) €12.50

➡ **Roma 72h** (valid for 72 hours) €18

➡ **CIS** (*carta integrata settimanale,* a weekly ticket) €24

Children under 10 travel free.

Buy tickets at *tabacchi,* newsstands and from vending machines at main bus stops and metro stations. They must be purchased before you start your journey and validated in the machines on buses, at the entrance gates to the metro or at train stations.

The **Roma Pass** (2/3 days €28/36) comes with a two/three-day travel pass valid within the city boundaries.

Buses from Termini

From Piazza dei Cinquecento outside Stazione Termini, buses run to all corners of the city.

DESTINATION	BUS NO
St Peter's Square	40/64
Piazza Venezia	40/64
Piazza Navona	40/64
Campo de' Fiori	40/64
Pantheon	40/64
Colosseum	75
Terme di Caracalla	714
Villa Borghese	910
Trastevere	H

(Spagna), and St Peter's (Ottaviano–San Pietro).

➡ Take line B for the Colosseum (Colosseo).

Bus

☑ **Best for...** Getting around the historic centre.

➡ Rome's buses and trams are run by **ATAC** (📞06 5 70 03; www.atac.roma.it).

➡ The main bus station is in front of Stazione Termini (Map p84, D2) on Piazza dei Cinquecento, where there's an **information booth** (🕑7.30am-8pm). Other important hubs are at Largo di Torre Argentina (Map p42, C5) and Piazza Venezia (Map p30, A1).

➡ Buses generally run from about 5.30am until midnight, with limited services throughout the night.

➡ Night buses are marked with an 'n' and bus stops have a blue owl symbol. The most useful routes:

n1 Follows the route of metro line A.

n2 Follows the route of metro line B.

n7 Piazzale Clodio, Corso del Rinascimento, Corso Vittorio Emanuele II, Largo di Torre Argentina, Piazza Venezia, Via Nazionale, Stazione Termini.

Tram

☑ **Best for...** Hopping over the river to Trastevere and for suburbs such as San Lorenzo and Pigneto.

The most useful tram routes for visitors:

Line 2 Runs north from Piazzale Flaminio.

Line 3 Ostiense, Testaccio, Colosseum, San Giovanni, San Lorenzo, Villa Borghese.

Line 8 Runs along Via Arenula to Trastevere.

Line 19 Connects Pigneto and San Lorenzo to Villa Borghese and the Vatican.

Taxi

☑ **Best for...** Late-night trips.

➡ Official licensed taxis are white with an ID number and *Roma Capitale* on the sides.

➡ Always go with the metered fare, never an arranged price (the set fares to and from the airports are exceptions).

➡ In town (within the ring road) flag fall is €3 from 6am to 10pm Monday to Saturday, €4.50 on Sundays and holidays, and €6.50 10pm to 6am. Then it's €1.10 per kilometre. Official rates are posted in taxis.

➡ You can hail a taxi, but it's easier to wait at a rank or phone for one. There are taxi ranks at the airports, Stazione Termini (Map p84, D2), Largo di Torre Argentina (Map p42, C5), Piazza della Repubblica (Map p84, C1), Piazza del Colosseo (Map p30, D4), Piazza Belli in Trastevere (Map p122, D3), and in the Vatican at Piazza Pio XII (Map p140, D4) and Piazza del Risorgimento (Map p140, D3).

➡ You can book a taxi by phoning the Comune di Roma's taxi line on ☎06 06 09 or calling a taxi company direct. Note that the meter starts running as soon as you book.

La Capitale (☎06 49 94)

Radio 3570 (☎06 35 70; www.3570.it)

Samarcanda (☎06 55 51; www.samarcanda.it)

Train

☑ **Best for...** Heading out of town to Ostia Antica.

Unless you're travelling beyond the main metropolitan area to places such as Ostia Antica, you shouldn't need to use Rome's suburban train network.

Essential Information

Business Hours

Banks 8.30am to 1.30pm and 2.45pm to 4.30pm Monday to Friday.

Bars and cafes 7.30am to 8pm, sometimes until 1am or 2am.

Shops 9am to 7.30pm or 10am to 8pm Monday to Saturday, some 11am to 7pm Sunday; smaller shops 9am to 1pm and 3.30pm to 7.30pm (or 4pm to 8pm) Monday to Saturday.

Clubs 10pm to 4am.

Restaurants Noon to 3pm and 7.30pm to 11pm (later in summer).

Discount Cards

☑ **Top Tip** If you use the Roma Pass for more expensive sights such as the Capitoline Museums, it's real value for money.

➡ EU citizens aged between 18 and 25 qualify for discounts at state-run museums; under 18s get in free. City-run museums are free for children under

six and discounted for six to 25 year olds. In all cases you'll need proof of age, ideally a passport or ID card.

➡ Discount cards can be purchased at any of the museums and monuments listed below. The Roma Pass is also available at tourist information points.

Classic Roma Pass (€36, valid for three days) Provides free admission to two museums or sites, as well as reduced entry to extra sites, unlimited city transport, and discounted entry to other exhibitions and events.

48-hour Roma Pass (€28, valid for 48 hours) Gives free admission to one museum or site and then as per the classic pass.

Archaeologia Card (adult/reduced €27.50/17.50, valid for seven days) Covers the Colosseum, Palatino, Roman Forum, Terme di Caracalla, Palazzo Altemps, Palazzo Massimo alle Terme, Terme di Diocleziano, Crypta Balbi, Mausoleo di Cecilia Metella and Villa Quintili.

Electricity

230V/50Hz

230V/50Hz

Emergencies

Ambulance (☑118)

Fire (☑115)

Police (☑112, 113)

Money

☑ **Top Tip** The daily cash withdrawal limit at ATMs is €250.

Italy uses the euro. Euro notes come in denominations of €500, €200, €100, €50, €20, €10 and €5; coins come in denominations of €2 and €1, and 50, 20, 10, five, two and one cents.

ATMs

➡ ATMs (known as *bancomat*) are widely available and most will accept cards tied to the Visa, MasterCard, Cirrus and Maestro systems.

➡ Always let your bank know when you're going abroad in case they block your card when payments appear from unusual locations.

Credit Cards

➡ Virtually all midrange and top-end hotels accept credit cards, as do most restaurants and large shops. Some cheaper *pensioni,* trattorias and pizzerias only accept cash. Don't rely on

credit cards at museums or galleries.

➡ Major cards such as Visa, MasterCard, Eurocard, Cirrus and Eurocheques are widely accepted. Amex is also recognised, although it's less common than Visa or MasterCard.

In case of emergency, call the following numbers to have your card blocked:

Amex (☑06 7290 0347)

Diners Club (☑800 393939)

MasterCard (☑800 870866)

Visa (☑800 819014)

Money Changers

➡ There are exchange booths at Stazione Termini and at Fiumicino and Ciampino airports.

➡ Take your passport or photo ID when exchanging money.

Tipping

➡ Service (*servizio*) is generally included in restaurants – if it's not, a euro or two is fine in pizzerias, 10% in restaurants. Tipping isn't necessary in bars.

➜ Rounding your taxi fare to the nearest euro will suffice.

➜ Tip porters about €4 at A-list hotels.

Public Holidays

Capodanno (New Year's Day) 1 January

Epifania (Epiphany) 6 January

Pasquetta (Easter Monday) March/April

Giorno della Liberazione (Liberation Day) 25 April

Festa del Lavoro (Labour Day) 1 May

Festa della Repubblica (Republic Day) 2 June

Festa dei Santi Pietro e Paolo (Feast of St Peter & St Paul) 29 June

Ferragosto (Feast of the Assumption) 15 August

Festa di Ognisanti (All Saints' Day) 1 November

Festa dell'Immacolata Concezione (Feast of the Immaculate Conception) 8 December

Natale (Christmas Day) 25 December

Festa di Santo Stefano (Boxing Day) 26 December

Safe Travel

☑ **Top Tip** Pickpockets go where the tourists go, so watch out around the most touristed and crowded areas of the city.

Rome is not a dangerous city, but petty theft is a problem. Watch out for pickpockets around the Colosseum, Piazza di Spagna, Piazza San Pietro, Stazione Termini and on crowded public transport – the 64 bus to the Vatican is notorious.

To minimise risks:

➜ Carry your day's spending money in a separate wallet.

➜ Wear your bag/camera strap across your body and away from the road – thieves on scooters can swipe a bag and be gone in seconds.

➜ Never drape your bag over an empty chair at a streetside cafe or put it where you can't see it.

➜ Always check your change to see you haven't been short-changed.

➜ In case of theft or loss, report the incident to the police within 24 hours and ask for a statement.

Telephone Services

Mobile Phones

➜ Italy uses the GSM 900/1800 cellular system, compatible with phones from the UK, Europe, Australia and most of Asia but not

Money-Saving Tips

➜ State-run museums are free on the first Sunday of the month.

➜ Fill up on art at Rome's churches – they're all free.

➜ Buy a Roma Pass if you want to blitz the sights.

➜ Lunch on sliced pizza and gelato; dine on bar snacks over an *aperitivo* (drink with bar buffet).

➜ Drink coffee standing at the bar rather than sitting at a table.

➜ Fill up on water at the drinking fountains known as *nasoni* (big noses).

Dos & Don'ts

Do...

➜ Greet people with a *buongiorno* (good morning) or *buonasera* (good evening).

➜ Dress the part – cover up when visiting churches and go smart when eating out.

➜ Eat pasta with a fork not a spoon, and keep your hands on the table not under it.

Don't...

➜ Feel you have to order everything on the menu. No one seriously expects you to eat a starter, pasta, second course and dessert.

➜ Order cappuccino after lunch or dinner. Well, OK, you can, but Romans don't.

➜ Wait for cars to stop at pedestrian crossings. You'll have to make the first move if you want to cross the road.

always with the North American GSM or CDMA systems – check with your service provider.

➜ Local SIM cards can be used in European, Australian and unlocked US phones. Other phones must be set to roaming. Buy prepaid SIM cards from **TIM** (www.tim.it), **Wind** (www.wind.it) or **Vodafone** (www.vodafone. it) outlets.

➜ Italian mobile-phone numbers begin with a three-digit prefix starting with 3.

Phone Codes

Italy's country code is ☏ 39, and the Rome area code is ☏ 06. The area code must be dialled, even when calling locally.

To call abroad from Italy, dial ☏ 00 before the country code.

Toilets

☑ **Top Tip** If there are no public toilets nearby, nip into a bar.

There are toilets at the Colosseum, St Peter's Square, Castel Sant'Angelo and Stazione Termini (€1).

Tourist Information

For phone enquiries, the Comune di Roma runs a free multilingual tourist information line (☏ 06 06 08).

There are information points at **Fiumicino** (Terminal 3, International Arrivals; ⏰ 8am-7.30pm) and **Ciampino** (International Arrivals, baggage claim area; ⏰ 9am-6.30pm) airports, and at locations across the city:

Piazza delle Cinque Lune (Map p42, B2; ⏰ 9.30am-7.15pm)

Stazione Termini (Map p84, D2; ⏰ 8am-7.45pm)

Fori Imperiali (Map p30, C2; Via dei Fori Imperiali; ⏰ 9.30am-7pm)

Via Marco Minghetti (Map p70, A4; Via Marco Minghetti; ⏰ 9.30am-7.15pm)

Via Nazionale (Map p84, A2; Via Nazionale; ⏰ 9.30am-7.15pm)

For information about the Vatican, contact the **Centro Servizi Pellegrini e Turisti** (Map p140, C4; ☏ 06 6988 1662; St Peter's Sq; ⏰ 8.30am-6pm Mon-Sat).

Useful websites include:

060608 (www.060608.it) Comprehensive information on sites, upcoming events, transport etc.

Roma Turismo (www.turismoroma.it) Rome's official tourist website with listings and up-to-date information.

Travellers with Disabilities

☑ **Top Tip** Metro line A is pretty much off-limits to wheelchairs, but bus 590 follows the same route.

➡ Cobbled streets, blocked pavements and tiny lifts make Rome a difficult city for travellers with physical disabilities.

➡ All stations on metro line B have wheelchair access except for Circo Massimo, Colosseo and Cavour.

➡ On line A, Ottaviano–San Pietro and Termini are equipped with lifts.

➡ Newer buses and trams have disabled access – bus stops show which routes are wheelchair accessible.

Visas

➡ EU citizens do not need a visa for Italy. Nationals of Australia, Canada, Israel, Japan, New Zealand, Switzerland and the USA do not need a visa for stays of up to 90 days.

➡ Italy is one of the 15 signatories of the Schengen Convention. The standard tourist visa for a Schengen country is valid for 90 days. You must apply for it in your country of residence. Get details on www.schengenvisainfo.com/tourist-schengen-visa.

Words right now
– liberated

Language

Regional dialects are an important part of identity in many parts of Italy, but you'll have no trouble being understood in Rome or anywhere else in the country if you stick to standard Italian, which is what we've also used in this chapter.

The sounds used in spoken Italian can all be found in English. If you read our pronunciation guides as if they were English, you'll be understood. The stressed syllables are indicated with italics. Note that *ai* is pronounced as in 'aisle', *ay* as in 'say', *ow* as in 'how', *dz* as the 'ds' in 'lids', and that *r* is a strong and rolled sound.

To enhance your trip with a phrasebook, visit **lonelyplanet.com**. Lonely Planet iPhone phrasebooks are available through the Apple App store.

Basics

Hello.
Buongiorno.   bwon·*jor*·no

Goodbye.
Arrivederci.   a·ree·ve·*der*·chee

How are you?
Come sta?   *ko*·me sta

Fine. And you?
Bene. E Lei?   *be*·ne e lay

Please.
Per favore.   per fa·*vo*·re

Thank you.
Grazie.   *gra*·tsye

Excuse me.
Mi scusi.   mee *skoo*·zee

Sorry.
Mi dispiace.   mee dees·*pya*·che

Yes./No.
Sì./No.   see/no

I don't understand.
Non capisco.   non ka·*pee*·sko

Do you speak English?
Parla inglese?   *par*·la een·*gle*·ze

Eating & Drinking

I'd like ...   *Vorrei ...*   vo·*ray* ...

  a coffee   *un caffè*   oon ka·*fe*

  a table   *un tavolo*   oon *ta*·vo·lo

  the menu   *il menù*   eel me·*noo*

  two beers   *due birre*   *doo*·e *bee*·re

What would you recommend?
Cosa mi   *ko*·za mee
consiglia?   kon·*see*·lya

Enjoy the meal!
Buon appetito!   bwon a·pe·*tee*·to

That was delicious!
Era squisito!   *e*·ra skwee·*zee*·to

Cheers!
Salute!   sa·*loo*·te

Can you bring me the bill, please?
Mi porta il conto,   mee *por*·ta eel *kon*·to
per favore?   per fa·*vo*·re

Shopping

I'd like to buy ...
Vorrei comprare ...   vo·*ray* kom·*pra*·re ...

I'm just looking.
Sto solo   sto *so*·lo
guardando.   gwar·*dan*·do

How much is this?
Quanto costa   kwan·to kos·ta
questo?   kwe·sto

It's too expensive.
È troppo caro/   e tro·po ka·ro/
cara. (m/f)   ka·ra

Emergencies

Help!
Aiuto!   a·yoo·to

Call the police!
Chiami la   kya·mee la
polizia!   po·lee·tsee·a

Call a doctor!
Chiami un   kya·mee oon
medico!   me·dee·ko

I'm sick.
Mi sento male.   mee sen·to ma·le

I'm lost.
Mi sono perso/   mee so·no per·so/
persa. (m/f)   per·sa

Where are the toilets?
Dove sono i   do·ve so·no ee
gabinetti?   ga·bee·ne·tee

Time & Numbers

What time is it?
Che ora è?   ke o·ra e

It's (two) o'clock.
Sono le (due).   so·no le (doo·e)

morning	*mattina*	ma·tee·na
afternoon	*pomeriggio*	po·me·ree·jo
evening	*sera*	se·ra
yesterday	*ieri*	ye·ree
today	*oggi*	o·jee
tomorrow	*domani*	do·ma·nee

1	*uno*	oo·no
2	*due*	doo·e
3	*tre*	tre
4	*quattro*	kwa·tro
5	*cinque*	cheen·kwe
6	*sei*	say
7	*sette*	se·te
8	*otto*	o·to
9	*nove*	no·ve
10	*dieci*	dye·chee
100	*cento*	chen·to
1000	*mille*	mee·le

Transport & Directions

Where's ...?
Dov'è ...?   do·ve ...

What's the address?
Qual'è   kwa·le
l'indirizzo?   leen·dee·ree·tso

Can you show me (on the map)?
Può mostrarmi   pwo mos·trar·mee
(sulla pianta)?   (soo·la pyan·ta)

At what time does the ... leave?
A che ora   a ke o·ra
parte ...?   par·te ...

Does it stop at ...?
Si ferma a ...?   see fer·ma a ...

How do I get there?
Come ci si   ko·me chee see
arriva?   a·ree·va

bus	*autobus*	ow·to·boos
ticket	*biglietto*	bee·lye·to
timetable	*orario*	o·ra·ryo
train	*il treno*	eel tre·no

Behind the Scenes

Send Us Your Feedback

We love to hear from travellers – your comments help make our books better. We read every word, and we guarantee that your feedback goes straight to the authors. Visit **lonelyplanet.com/contact** to submit your updates and suggestions.

Note: We may edit, reproduce and incorporate your comments in Lonely Planet products such as guidebooks, websites and digital products, so let us know if you don't want your comments reproduced or your name acknowledged. For a copy of our privacy policy visit lonelyplanet.com/privacy.

Our Readers

Many thanks to the travellers who used the last edition and wrote to us with helpful hints, useful advice and interesting anecdotes:

Alexis Mooney, Andreas Müller, Edgar Vandepas, Jan Musil, Janet Weston, Michael Wyre, Nikolaj Mortensen, Robyn Matheson

Duncan's Thanks

A big thank you to Abi Blasi for her great suggestions and to Anna Tyler for her unstinting support. For their help with research grazie to Silvia Prosperi, Barbara Lessona, and the team at The Roman Guy. As always, a big hug to Lidia and the boys, Ben and Nick.

Acknowledgments

Cover Photograph: Colosseum, Sandra Raccanello/4Corners
Photograph on pp4–5: Roman Forum, tupungato/Getty

This Book

This 4th edition of Lonely Planet's *Pocket Rome* guidebook was coordinated by Duncan Garwood, and researched and written by Duncan and Abigail Blasi. The previous edition was also written by Duncan. This guidebook was produced by the following people:

Destination Editor Anna Tyler **Product Editors** Briohny Hooper, Vicky Smith **Coordinating Editor** Rosie Nicholson **Senior Cartographer** Anthony Phelan **Book Designer** Virginia Moreno **Assisting Editor** Kate Evans **Cartographer** Julie Dodkins **Cover Researcher** Naomi Parker

Thanks to Shahara Ahmed, Anita Bahn, Kate Chapman, Mark Griffiths, Andi Jones, Anne Mason, Claire Murphy, Karyn Noble, Martine Power, Kirsten Rawlings, Samantha Russell-Tulip, Dianne Schallmeiner, Angela Tinson, Lauren Wellicome, Tony Wheeler, Amanda Williamson

Index

See also separate subindexes for:

😣 **Eating p190**

🍷 **Drinking p190**

✪ **Entertainment p191**

🛍 **Shopping p191**

A

Accademia Filarmonica Romana 169
accommodation 174-5
ambulance 180
ancient Rome area 22-35, **30**
   drinking 35
   food 33, 35
   itineraries 23
   sights 24-9, 31-3
   transport 23
aperitivo 129
Appian Way 10, 92, 95
architecture 48, 74, 162-3
Arco di Costantino 25
Arco di Settimio Severo 27
Arco di Tito 28
Arco Farnese 41
Area Archeologica del Teatro di Marcello e del Portico D'Ottavia 46
area codes 182
art 48, 164-5, *see also individual artists*
ATMs 180
Auditorium Parco della Musica 148

Sights 000
Map Pages **000**

Augustus, Emperor 34
Aventino 108-15, **110**

B

Barcaccia 57
baroque architecture 48, 74, 162-3
baroque art 48, 164-5
bars 161, *see also individual neighbourhoods*, Drinking subindex
Basilica di Massenzio 28
Basilica di San Clemente 101
Basilica di San Giovanni in Laterano 11, 98-9
Basilica di San Lorenzo Fuori le Mura 79
Basilica di San Paolo Fuori le Mura 107
Basilica di San Pietro in Vincoli 85
Basilica di San Sebastiano 93
Basilica di Santa Cecilia in Trastevere 123
Basilica di Santa Maria in Trastevere 11, 118-19
Basilica di Santa Maria Maggiore 85
Basilica di Santa Maria Sopra Minerva 45

Basilica di Santa Sabina 111
Basilica di SS Quattro Coronati 101
bathrooms 182
Battistero 101
Bernini 48, 74
bike tours 171
Bioparco 170
Borromini 48, 74
bus tours 171
bus travel 178
business hours 179

C

Campo de' Fiori 46-7
Capitoline Museums 31
Caravaggio 44, 48, 164
Casa delle Vestali 28
Case Romane 103
Castel Sant'Angelo 142
Catacombe di San Callisto 94
Catacombe di San Sebastiano 93
Catacombe di Santa Domitilla 94
catacombs 94
Celio, *see* San Giovanni & Celio
cell phones 181-2
Centrale Montemartini 107

Centro Storico area 36-53, **42-3**
   drinking 50-2
   entertainment 52
   food 47-50
   itineraries 37, 40-1, **40**
   shopping 52-3
   sights 38-9, 44-7
   transport 37
Chiesa del Gesù 44-5
Chiesa della Trinità dei Monti 57
Chiesa di San Carlo alle Quattro Fontane 71
Chiesa di San Francesco d'Assisi a Ripa 123
Chiesa di San Luigi dei Francesi 44
Chiesa di San Pietro in Montorio 123
Chiesa di Santa Maria del Popolo 59
Chiesa di Santa Maria della Vittoria 71
Chiesa di Santa Maria in Aracoeli 31
Chiesa di Santa Prassede 85
Chiesa di Sant'Andrea al Quirinale 72
Chiesa di Sant'Ignazio di Loyola 45-6
Chiesa di Santo Stefano Rotondo 102
children, travel with 170

Chiostro del Bramante 40

Christina, Queen of Sweden 139

Cimitero Acattolico per gli Stranieri 112

Cimitero di Campo Verano 79

climate 174

clubs 161, see also Drinking & Entertainment subindexes

Colonna dell'Immacolata 57

Colonna di Foca 28

Colosseum 8, 24-5

Convento dei Cappuccini 74

costs 16, 179-81

credit cards 180

Curia 27

currency 180

D

dangers 181

disabilities, travellers with 183

Domus Aurea 85

Donation of Constantine 102

drinking 129, 161, see also individual neighbourhoods, Drinking subindex

E

Ekberg, Anita 73

electricity 180

emergencies 180

Esposizione Universale di Roma (EUR) 163

Esquilino, see Monti & Esquilino

etiquette 182

Explora – Museo dei Bambini di Roma 170

F

Fellini, Federico 73

Festa de' Noantri 124

film 73, 168-9

Fontana del Mascherone 41

Fontana del Quattro Fiumi 44

food 114, 158-9, see also individual neighbourhoods, Eating subindex

aperitivo 129

gelato 76

quinto quarto 114

free sights 160

G

Gagosian Gallery 72

Galleria Colonna 72

Galleria d'Arte Moderna 72

Galleria Doria Pamphilj 44

Galleria Nazionale d'Arte Antica di Palazzo Corsini 124

Galleria Nazionale d'Arte Antica: Palazzo Barberini 71

Galleria Nazionale d'Arte Moderna e Contemporanea 148

galleries 48, 164-5, see also individual galleries

Garbatella 107

gay travellers 172

gelato 76

Gianicolo, see Trastevere & Gianicolo

H

highlights 8-11, 12-13

historic centre, see Centro Storico area

history 34, 156-7

holidays 181

I

Il Vittoriano 32

Imperial Forums 32

Isola Tiberina 46

Italian language 184-5

itineraries 14-15, 40-1, 78-9, 106-7, 120-1, 152-5, see also individual neighbourhoods

J

Jewish Ghetto 46

K

Keats, John 59-60, 112

Keats-Shelley House 59-60

L

La Dolce Vita 73

La grande bellezza 73

language 184-5

Lapis Niger 27

lesbian travellers 172

local life 12-13

M

MACRO Testaccio 112

Mausoleo di Cecilia Metella 93

Mausoleo di Romolo 93

MAXXI 148

Mercati di Traiano Museo dei Fori Imperiali 32

metro 177-8

Michelangelo 48, 132, 136, 164

Mithraism 104

mobile phones 181-2

money 16, 179-81

Monte Testaccio 112

Monti & Esquilino 80-91, **84**

drinking 89

entertainment 89-90

food 87-9

itineraries 81

shopping 90-1

sights 82-3, 85-7

transport 81

Museo Carlo Bilotti 148

Museo dell'Ara Pacis 59

Museo delle Cere 170

Museo e Galleria Borghese 147

Museo Ebraico di Roma 46

Museo Nazionale d'Arte Orientale 86

Museo Nazionale delle Arti del XXI Secolo (MAXXI) 148

Museo Nazionale Etrusco di Villa Giulia 147

Museo Nazionale Romano: Crypta Balbi 46

Museo Nazionale Romano: Palazzo Altemps 44

Museo Nazionale Romano: Palazzo Massimo alle Terme 10, 82-3

Sights 000
Map Pages **000**

Museo Nazionale Romano: Terme di Diocleziano 85-6

Museo Pio-Clementino 133

Museo Storico Artistico 139

museums 164-5, see also individual museums

music 168-9, see also Entertainment subindex

N

nightlife 161, see also Drinking & Entertainment subindexes

O

opening hours 179

Orto Botanico 124

Ostia Antica 157

Ostiense 106-7, **106**

P

Palatino 31

Palazzo del Quirinale 72

Palazzo della Civiltà del Lavoro 163

Palazzo delle Esposizioni 86

Palazzo Farnese 46

Palazzo Laterano 101

Palazzo Spada 41

Palazzo Venezia 33

Pantheon 9, 38-9

Parco Savello 111

passeggiata 61

Pastificio Cerere 79

Piazza del Campidoglio 31

Piazza del Popolo 59

Piazza del Quirinale 71

Piazza della Repubblica 87

Piazza di Spagna 11, 56-7

Piazza Mignanelli 57

Piazza Navona 44

Piazza Pasquino 41

Piazza Santa Maria in Trastevere 121

Piazza Vittorio Emanuele II 86

Pietà 137

Pigneto 78-9, **78**

Pinacoteca 133

planning 16-17

police 180

Ponte Sant'Angelo 142

pope, the 142

Porta Magica 86

Prati, see Vatican City & Prati

Priorato dei Cavalieri di Malta 111

public holidays 181

Q

Quirinale, see Trevi & the Quirinale

R

Renaissance architecture 48, 162

Renaissance art 48, 164

Roman Empire 34, 152

Roman Forum 10, 26-9, **29**

Roman Holiday 73

Romulus & Remus 32

S

safety 181

San Giovanni & Celio 96-105, **100**

drinking 104-5

food 103-4

itineraries 97

shopping 105

sights 98-9, 101-3

transport 97

San Lorenzo 78-9, **78**

San Paolo 106-7, **106**

Santuario della Scala Santa & Sancta Sanctorum 101

Scavi Archeologici di Ostia Antica 157

Scuderie Papali al Quirinale 72

Shelley, Percy 59-60, 112

shopping 166-7, see also individual neighbourhoods, Shopping subindex

Sistine Chapel 134

Spanish Steps 11, 56-7

St Peter's Basilica 9, 136-9, **138**

St Peter's Square 142

T

taxis 178-9

Teatro Olimpico 169

telephone services 181-2

Tempietto di Bramante 123

Tempio di Castore e Polluce 28

Tempio di Giulio Cesare 27

Tempio di Saturno 28

Tempio di Vesta 28

Terme di Caracalla 111

Testaccio 108-15, **110**

theatre 168-9

time 16

tipping 180

toilets 182

Tomb of St Peter 139

top sights 8-11

tourist information 182

tours 171

train travel, see metro

trams 178

transport 176-9, see also individual neighbourhoods

Trastevere & Gianicolo 116-29, **122**

drinking 126-7

entertainment 127

food 124-6

itineraries 117, 120-1, **120**

shopping 128

sights 118-19, 123-4

transport 117

Trevi & the Quirinale 66-77, **70**

drinking 77

entertainment 77

food 74-7

itineraries 67

shopping 77

sights 68-9, 71-4

transport 67

Trevi Fountain 11, 68-9

Tridente 54-65, **58**

drinking 63-4

food 60-2

itineraries 55

shopping 64-5

sights 56-7, 59-60

transport 55

V

Vatican City & Prati 130-45, **140-1**

drinking 144-5

entertainment 145

food 142-4

itineraries 131

shopping 145

sights 132-9, 142

transport 131

Vatican Grottoes 139
Vatican Museums 9, 132-5, **135**
vestal virgins 28
Via Appia Antica 10, 92, 95
Via dei Condotti 60
Via del Governo Vecchio 41
Via del Porto Fluviale 107
Via Giulia 41
Via Margutta 59
Via Sacra 27
Villa Borghese 10, 146-9, 149
Villa Celimontana 102
Villa di Massenzio 93
Villa Farnesina 123
Villa Medici 60
visas 183

W
walking tours 12-13, 152-5, 171, **153**, **155**
weather 174
websites 174-5

🍽 Eating

A
Al Gran Sasso 61
Al Moro 76
Alfredo e Ada 41
Alimentari Pannella Carmela 35
Andreotti 107
Armando al Pantheon 47
Aroma 103

B
Babette 62
Baccano 75
Buccone 62

C
Cafè Cafè 103
Caffè delle Arti 147
Caffè Propaganda 104
Casa Bleve 49
Casa Conti 62
Casa Coppelle 47
Checchino dal 1887 114
Ciuri Ciuri 88
Colline Emiliane 74
Cul de Sac 50

D
Da Corrado 126
Da Felice 113
Da Michele 75
Da Olindo 121
Da Valentino 88
Dei Gracchi 62
Del Frate 144
Ditirambo 49

E
Eataly 107
Enoteca Regionale Palatium 60

F
Fatamorgana 60
Fatamorgana – Trastevere 124
Flavio al Velavevodetto 112
Forno di Campo de' Fiori 49
Forno Roscioli 49

G
Gelarmony 144
Gina 61
Glass Hostaria 125

H
Hostaria Dino e Tony 144

I
Il Bocconcino 103
Il Chianti 75
Il Gelato 113
Il Margutta RistorArte 62
Il Sorpasso 144
Imàgo 61

L
La Ciambella 47
La Gensola 124
L'Asino d'Oro 87
Le Mani in Pasta 125
Le Tamerici 76
Li Rioni 103

N
Nanà Vini e Cucina 76

O
Open Colonna 87

P
Panella l'Arte del Pane 88
Paris 125
Pasticceria Regoli 88
Pastificio 64
Pianostrada Laboratorio di Cucina 125
Pizzarium 142
Pizzeria Da Remo 113
Pizzeria Ivo 125
Pommidoro 79

Q
Qui Non se More Mai 93

R
Ristorante L'Arcangelo 143
Ristorante Roof Garden Circus 35
Romeo 143

S
Said 79
San Crispino 76
Supplizio 47

T
Taverna dei Quaranta 104
Temakinho 88
Terre e Domus 33
Trapizzino 113
Trattoria Monti 87

V
Velavevodetto Ai Quiriti 143
Venchi 49

🍷 Drinking

0,75 35

A
Ai Tre Scalini 89

B
Bar San Calisto 121
Bar Stuzzichini 120
Barnum Cafe 50
Big Star 126

C
Caffè Capitolino 35
Caffè Greco 64

Sights **000**
Map Pages **000**

Caffè Sant'Eustachio 50
Canova Tadolini 64
Cavour 313 35
Circus 51
Coming Out 104
Co.So 79

D

Da Biagio 126
Doppiozeroo 107

E

Etablì 50

F

Fafiuché 89
Freni e Frizioni 121

I

Il Barretto 127
Il Goccetto 51
Il Pentagrappolo 104

L

La Barrique 89
La Bottega del Caffè 89
La Casa del Caffè Tazza d'Oro 50
La Mescita 126
La Scena 63
L'Alibi 115
Linari 115

M

Ma Che Siete Venuti a Fà 126
Makasar 145
Moma 77

N

Necci 79
No.Au 51

O

Ombre Rosse 126
Open Baladin 41

P

Passaguai 144

R

Rec 23 114

S

Salotto 42 52
Sciascia Caffè 144
Stravinskij Bar 63

Entertainment

Alexanderplatz 145
Big Mama 121
Blackmarket 90
Charity Café 90
ConteStaccio 115
Fonclea 145
Goa 107
Gregory's 77
La Saponeria 107
Lettere Caffè Gallery 127
Neo Club 107
Nuovo Sacher 121
Teatro Argentina 52
Teatro dell'Opera di Roma 89

Shopping

101 91

A

Abito 91
Antica Caciara Trasteverina 128
Antica Manufattura Cappelli 145

B

Borini 53
Bottega di Marmoraro 64
Bottega Pio La Torre 53

C

Confetteria Moriondo & Gariglio 52
C.U.C.I.N.A. 65

D

Danielle 64

E

Enoteca Costantini 145

F

Fabio Piccioni 90
Fausto Santini 65
Fendi 64

G

Galleria Alberto Sordi 77
Giacomo Santini 91

I

Ibiz – Artigianato in Cuoio 52

L

La Bottega del Cioccolato 90
Le Artigiane 53
Lucia Odescalchi 77
Luna & L'Altra 53

M

Mercato Monti Urban Market 90

N

Nardecchia 53
Nuovo Mercato di Testaccio 115

O

Officina della Carta 128
Officina Profumo Farmaceutica di Santa Maria Novella 52

P

Pelletteria Nives 65
Porta Portese Market 128

R

Roma-Store 128

S

SBU 41
Scala Quattordici Clothing 128
Sermoneta 65
Soul Food 105
Spot 90

T

Tina Sondergaard 90

U

Underground 77

V

Vertecchi Art 65
Via dei Condotti 57
Via del Boschetto 90
Via del Governo Vecchio 41
Via Sannio 105
Volpetti 115

Our Writers

Duncan Garwood

A Brit travel writer based in the Castelli Romani hills just outside Rome, Duncan moved to the Italian capital just in time to see the new millennium in at the Colosseum. He has since clocked up hundreds of kilometres walking around his adopted hometown and exploring its hidden corners. He wrote the previous edition of this book and has worked on the last six editions of the Rome city guide as well as a whole host of LP Italy publications. He has also written on Italy for newspapers and magazines. Read more about Duncan at: lonelyplanet.com/members/duncangarwood

Contributing Writer

Abigail Blasi contributed to the Tridente, Trevi & the Quirinale, Monti & Esquilino, San Lorenzo & Pigneto and Trastevere & Gianicolo chapters.

Published by Lonely Planet Publications Pty Ltd
ABN 36 005 607 983
4th edition – Jan 2016
ISBN 978 1 74220 8862
© Lonely Planet 2016 Photographs © as indicated 2016
10 9 8 7 6 5 4 3 2
Printed in China